CONGRESS, THE EXECUTIVE, AND FOREIGN POLICY

CONGRESS,
THE EXECUTIVE, AND
FOREIGN POLICY

by FRANCIS O. WILCOX

Published for the
Council on Foreign Relations
by
Harper & Row, Publishers
New York, Evanston, San Francisco
London

The Council on Foreign Relations is a nonprofit institution devoted to the study of political, economic, and strategic problems as related to American foreign policy. It takes no stand, expressed or implied, on American policy.

The authors of books published under the auspices of the Council are responsible for their statements of fact and expressions of opinion. The Council is responsible only for determining that they should be presented to the public.

For a list of Council publications see pages 177–179.

CONGRESS, THE EXECUTIVE, AND FOREIGN POLICY. Copyright © 1971 by *Council on Foreign Relations, Inc. All rights reserved. Printed in the United States of America. No part of this book may be used or reproduced in any manner whatsoever without written permission except in the case of brief quotations embodied in critical articles and reviews. For information address Harper & Row, Publishers, Inc., 49 East 33rd Street, New York, N.Y. 10016. Published simultaneously in Canada by Fitzhenry & Whiteside Limited, Toronto.*

FIRST EDITION

STANDARD BOOK NUMBER: 06-014651-6

LIBRARY OF CONGRESS CATALOG CARD NUMBER: 74-160654

To the students of The Johns Hopkins School of Advanced International Studies and others of the younger generation, who are preparing themselves to help in the development of a better world order.

Policy Books of the Council on Foreign Relations

The purpose of the Council's series of Policy Books has been to present to the public and to responsible officials in relatively brief compass the thinking of particularly qualified authors on international issues of major importance to the United States. The subject of the roles of the Congress and of the executive branch in foreign policy may not fit the strict definition of an international issue, but there is no doubt whatever of its crucial bearing on the question whether the United States can have an effective policy on any international problem. Vietnam has illustrated the point with utmost clarity. But its roots go far back in our history, to the Constitution itself, and it will be with us long after Vietnam. It is, therefore, a fitting subject for an extended essay in this series.

The value of a book such as this depends uniquely on the experience and qualities of its author. Especially in these past few years, when the subject of legislative-executive relations in the field of foreign policy has generated heated views by participants on both sides and by their advocates and defenders as well, an analysis which is both informed and penetrating is very much needed and very hard to find. The Council is fortunate in having persuaded Dr. Francis O. Wilcox, Dean of the School of Advanced International Studies of The Johns Hopkins University, to undertake the task. He combines professional scholarship with a practical experience which saw him on both sides of the line, as Chief of Staff of the Senate Foreign Relations Committee and later as an Assistant Secretary of State. Here he draws on that experience as well as his more recent close study of the battering the executive-legislative relationship has taken from the storm and stress of the Vietnam war. He goes beyond the constitutional aspects to the heart of the problem, which has to do with substance as well as process, and makes some proposals of his own for restoring the balance on which our governmental system depends.

The author wishes to thank the many members of Congress and the executive branch who willingly shared their ideas with him. He also had the benefit of the advice of a small group which met for a day at the Council to review and discuss his manuscript. He and the Council are grateful to the following individuals who either attended the review meeting or gave their views and comments directly to him: William J. Barnds, Douglas Cater, Robert G. Gard, Jr., Ernest A. Gross, Robert W. Hartley, H. Field Haviland, Pat M. Holt, Philip C. Jessup, Joseph E. Johnson, David W. MacEachron, Carl M. Marcy, Charles Burton Marshall, Alexander Schnee, Robert W. Valkenier, William R. Usher, Albert C. Westphal and Kurtin Winsor, Jr. This is, however, Francis Wilcox's book. Neither the Council nor any group has responsibility for its statements of fact or opinion. The Council does take responsibility for the decision to publish it as a contribution to thinking on a relationship vital to the development of sound and manageable foreign policies.

John C. Campbell
Editor

Contents

CONGRESS, THE EXECUTIVE, AND FOREIGN POLICY

Chapter I

Introduction: Congress Seeks a New Role

In March 1968, the widely-publicized television "confrontation" between Secretary of State Dean Rusk and Senator J. William Fulbright, Chairman of the Senate Foreign Relations Committee, over the war in South Vietnam, marked a significant point in recent American history. Some say it was merely a case of the Senate reasserting itself after long years of playing a relatively minor role in foreign policy. Drew Pearson, with his flair for the dramatic, put it this way: "Fulbright hearings end a decade as Automatic Rubber Stamp." Regardless of the interpretation one puts on the event, this much is clear: it represented the first time since World War II that the leaders of the Senate openly and vigorously disagreed with their President on a really vital question in the field of foreign relations.

From the earliest days of the Republic, the proper constitutional role of Congress in foreign policy has been a matter of dispute. At times, this dispute has been limited to scholars; at other times, it has embroiled Congress itself, the executive branch, and large segments of the public in the most acerbic and serious feuds carrying the gravest constitutional implications.

The argument over the relative roles of Congress and the executive branch in the making of foreign policy rises and falls in rough correlation to the argument over the substance of the policy itself. When there has been a reasonable consensus about

America's objectives in the world and how to achieve them, the congressional role has been played reasonably well and caused little debate. When this consensus has not existed, relations have become more abrasive and have tended to break down.

In fact, the years since 1965 have seen the American people divided as never before in their history over issues of foreign policy. The principal source of division has been the war in Southeast Asia, but the national debate that has ensued has brought to the surface deeper questions concerning fundamental national interests and the role of the United States in a rapidly changing world.

Although things are never quite as bad as they seem in Washington, the doubts and divisions which have beset the American people have naturally been reflected in Congress. They have led to a re-examination by Congress not only of the substance of American foreign policy but also of the procedures by which foreign policy is made and particularly of the congressional role in these procedures.

Perhaps the point is best made in a comparison of the reversed roles of some of the participants in two of the Senate's great debates on foreign policy held almost two decades apart, in 1951 and 1970.

A Confusing Picture

In 1951 the issue involved sending ground troops to Europe and the President's power to do so without the express approval of Congress. The leader of the effort to circumscribe the President's power was Senator Kenneth Wherry of Nebraska, the Republican floor leader. Opposing him were Senator Tom Connally of Texas, Chairman of the Foreign Relations Committee; Connally's junior colleague, Senator J. William Fulbright of Arkansas; and most of the Senate "establishment," including Majority Leader Ernest McFarland of Arizona. One of the points at issue was whether or not Secretary of State Dean Acheson had misled the Senate about the Truman administration's intentions to send American troops to Europe in order to give substance to our NATO commitments.

In 1970 the Senate had another great debate on the same issue of the President's power to send troops abroad: this time the destination of the troops in question was Cambodia instead of Europe. In the forefront of those seeking to limit the President were Senator Fulbright, by that time chairman of the Foreign Relations Committee, and Majority Leader Mike Mansfield. Seeking to protect the President's powers was Senator Robert Griffin of Michigan, the Republican Whip. And one of the points at issue was whether or not Secretary of State William P. Rogers had misled the Senate about the Nixon administration's intentions to use American troops in Cambodia.

Finally, it is worth recalling that Richard Nixon, who as President precipitated the 1970 debate by sending troops into Cambodia, had as a Senator from California voted against sending them to Europe. And 20 years after they were sent, his administration was stoutly resisting rather persistent congressional pressure— from Mansfield, among others—to bring some of them home.

In each of these instances, obviously, attitudes toward the substance of the policy affected attitudes toward the constitutional question of who had the power to do what. Or, as the *Christian Science Monitor* put it in the spring of 1970:

This spring the land is filled . . . with a resounding chorus demanding that the United States Senate reassert its "right" over foreign policy. . . .

Fine. We, too, more than once have suggested that it would be a healthy development if the Senate were to show more initiative, exercise more leadership, donate more thinking to foreign affairs. It was clearly the intention of the Founding Fathers that both the presidency and Congress should have their say.

But, hold on a moment. Which Senate are we speaking of? Are we talking of the Senate which has over and over again balked at constructive foreign initiative, crippled foreign efforts, ignored foreign opportunities? Are we talking of the Senate which blocked American entry into the League of Nations, held back full support for the World Court, is presently cutting back further and further on foreign aid, which has no hesitation over passing resolutions mixing in the affairs of other countries for political rather than diplomatic reasons?

Of course, this is not the Senate which today's "strengthen-the-Senate" advocates have in mind. They visualize an upper chamber full of wisdom and goodwill, a bulwark of reason and foresight in a reckless world. In short, they dream of a Senate which will hew to their own concept of where foreign policy should go and how it should be conducted.

But, alas, in the world of politics we must expect the bad with the good, the unwise with the far-seeing, the heedless with the prudent. A Senate which has asserted an iron hand over the President on Southeast Asia, might also be inclined to assert an equally hard fist where other very different issues are concerned.[1]

At the same time, there is in Congress a substantial group which takes an institutional view of congressional prerogatives quite unrelated to the merits of the particular issue. One could scarcely find two men of more diverse policy views than the late Representative L. Mendel Rivers (Democrat of South Carolina), former Chairman of the House Armed Services Committee, and Senator Fulbright. Yet witnesses before Rivers' Armed Services Committee were normally confronted with a conspicuous sign quoting from the Constitution: "The Congress shall have Power . . . To make Rules for the Government and Regulation of the land and naval Forces . . ." And Fulbright has been in the forefront of the growing group of Senators demanding greater respect for the congressional power to declare war and for the Senate's power to give (or withhold) its advice and consent to treaties.

One of the important differences between Rivers and Fulbright is that, while they agreed on a larger and more important role for Congress, Rivers seemed to want to use that role to free the uniformed military from the control of Pentagon civilians and Fulbright wants to use it to curb both the military and the civilians in the defense establishment.

1. "Will the real Senate stand up?" *Christian Science Monitor,* May 29–June 1, 1970.

Either case, however, is illustrative of a growing self-assertiveness on the part of Congress. Together they indicate one of the reasons why that self-assertiveness is not more effective—precisely because Congress is at least as divided as the country is over the underlying substantive issues of foreign policy.

Furthermore, although the pages of the *Congressional Record* for the last few years are filled with learned (and some not so learned) discussions of the relative constitutional powers of Congress and the President, a substantial number of members of Congress who strongly disapprove of the Vietnam war have been unwilling to use the ultimate power of Congress—that is, the power of the purse—to end the war by cutting off the money needed to carry it on.

Notwithstanding all this, a tide has clearly been running toward a larger congressional role in foreign policy and, perhaps more importantly, toward a new conception of that role. The most dramatic evidence of this trend is seen in the disposition of a substantial minority of the Senate vigorously to question Defense Department appropriations, something which would have been almost unthinkable as recently as a decade ago. Defense Department authorization and appropriation bills (running into many billions of dollars), which used to breeze through the Senate in an afternoon, now tie that body in knots for weeks on end.

This trend is much more noticeable in the Senate than in the House. The reasons are obscure, but a variety suggest themselves. With its larger size and tighter rules and procedures, the House has traditionally been a more disciplined body, much more amenable to the wishes and direction of its leadership, than the Senate. Moreover, the Constitution gives the Senate greater responsibilities in foreign policy and likewise, through longer terms and more heterogeneous constituencies, gives its members a greater degree of political independence. Nor should one overlook the obvious fact that in recent years the Senate especially has become the leading arena in the country for presidential politics. With so many Senators casting covetous eyes on the White House, it is inevitable that the Senate should play a more aggressive role—especially with respect to foreign policy questions like Vietnam and the Middle East, which are of vital importance to our nation. Finally, perhaps as much a result of historical accident as anything else, there is a substantial difference in the leading personalities of the two bodies. The Senate Majority Leader, Majority Whip, and Chairman of the Foreign Relations Committee all take quite different views, not only of the substance of foreign policy but also of their role in making it, from those of their counterparts in the House.

The striking differences between Senator Fulbright and Representative Thomas E. Morgan, Chairman of the House Foreign Affairs Committee, in this regard are certainly illustrative. Dr. Morgan describes himself as "only the quarterback not the coach of the team" which handles our foreign policy. He looks upon his committee as a subordinate partner or perhaps as a board of directors in a permanent alliance with the executive branch, and he believes the committee should normally support the administration's policy positions. In his rather modest way, he obviously prefers a low-profile approach to world affairs both for himself and his committee.

In contrast, Senator Fulbright has carved out for himself and his committee a much more assertive role. He believes the Congress, as a co-equal branch of government, has unwisely allowed some of its powers to lapse and that they should be reclaimed. In some quarters in Washington he has been looked upon as "the great dissenter." As leader of the so-called doves in the Senate and as chairman of the committee, he has considered it his duty not only to challenge the administration on policies he considers unwise, but even to take such issues to the American people whenever he believes this necessary.

The two men became chairmen of their respective committees in 1959, and to a certain extent the committees they lead reflect their differences in attitude and personality.[2]

2. See *1970 Congressional Quarterly, Fact Sheet,* November 20, 1970.

A Look Backward

This increasing congressional assertiveness with respect to foreign policy, though far from universally shared on Capitol Hill, is nonetheless one of the dominant political facts of our time and needs to be put in historical perspective. For present purposes, it suffices to begin with the aftermath of World War I. The Senate asserted itself in such fashion as to reject United States membership in the League of Nations and the World Court. In effect, largely because of the Senate's negative reaction, the United States almost turned its back on the world community in the 1920s and 1930s. Later on, dominated by much the same philosophy, the Senate joined with the House to pass the Neutrality Acts.

World War II brought a massive change in American thinking. It became fashionable to point to the errors of congressional foreign policy actions during the interwar period, and from this it was but a short step to presuming the existence of some kind of superior wisdom in the State Department and the White House. Wars inherently demand the exercise of greater executive powers, but the trend back toward the White House was in evidence even before Pearl Harbor. The bold actions of President Franklin D. Roosevelt in 1940 and 1941—in consummating the destroyers-for-bases deal with Winston Churchill, in sending troops to Iceland, in arming merchant ships (something which Wilson thought he did not have authority to do in 1917)—all rested on controversial constitutional grounds. They were, indeed, vigorously challenged by a minority in Congress. But they were supported by a majority, including the congressional leadership, not so much on grounds that the President had the constitutional authority to take these steps as that the national interest required them to be taken in a time of crisis. Those who opposed Roosevelt's policies argued that they required congressional approval. Those who supported them found it more convenient to avoid the trials and tribulations of congressional debate by finding constitutional power for the President to act as he did. It was neither the first nor the last time that ends and means of foreign policy have been confused; sometimes unwittingly, sometimes deliberately.

In the atmosphere of World War II, and out of the turbulent history of the interwar period, there developed a great resolve on the part of key figures at both ends of Pennsylvania Avenue that the post-World War I return to isolationism would not be repeated in the aftermath of World War II. Thus began the period of extraordinary executive-legislative cooperation which characterized the late 1940s and extended, with some erosion, into the middle 1960s. This period saw Senate approval, by overwhelming votes, of the United Nations Charter, the peace treaties with Italy and the satellite states, and the whole network of regional security treaties—the Rio Treaty, NATO, SEATO, and others. It saw congressional approval, in most cases by overwhelming votes, of aid to Greece and Turkey, the Marshall Plan, the Point Four Program, and U. S. participation in a wide variety of U.N. specialized agencies. It saw congressional acquiescence in the Korean War, which was fought entirely by executive fiat, supported by congressional appropriations.

During this period the bipartisan approach to foreign policy reached its zenith. Even at its zenith, however, bipartisanship had a very limited application. In effect, it applied principally to those major policy issues involving treaties and legislation on which congressional action was necessary. It left relatively untouched that vast array of diplomatic and military decisions which the President must make and which normally lie outside the legislative orbit. But it imparted a certain stability and unity of purpose to our policy that proved most helpful in the formative years of the postwar era. I can recall only one instance during the entire Eightieth Congress, for example, when the Senate Foreign Relations Committee failed to arrive at a unanimous vote on an important policy question.

All this was possible because thinking in the executive branch and in the pertinent quarters of Congress was along roughly parallel lines, and there was thorough consultation. There was, in other words, a general consensus about the basic elements of

American policy and the process by which policy should be developed. It was, to be sure, far from total, as the war in Korea clearly demonstrated. The Senate barely upheld the President on sending American troops to Europe in 1951, and then only after the great debate noted above. Senator Joseph McCarthy and his supporters involved us in a national and international scandal whose wounds were slow to heal but which now appears, from a distance of two decades, as a temporary aberration.

The general consensus of the 1940s and 1950s was shared not only by the executive branch and most members of Congress, but by the American public as well. It embraced, in broad terms, both the means and the ends of foreign policy. Then it was seriously damaged in the 1960s. Many factors entered into this development, but the most important by far was the war in Vietnam.

Congress Seeks a New Role

The thinking of congressional opponents to the Vietnam war moved progressively from private doubts and opinion to open conviction and even to near obsession. By no means did the process evolve uniformly for all opponents, nor did it lead them all to the ultimate, obsessive stage. But it did lead most of them to re-examine how the United States got embroiled in Vietnam in the first place, and to reconsider the proper constitutional roles of the President and Congress with respect to foreign policy. It was perfectly natural that these opponents, including some of the most prominent and articulate members of the Senate, should attempt to curb the President's powers by claiming greater prerogatives for Congress.

In this attempt they have encountered many frustrations, not the least of which is that many other members of Congress, especially in the House, either do not agree with them or are unwilling to support them. But beyond this, the most troublesome and frustrating question has been how, in this world of the 1970s, Congress can participate meaningfully in the making of American foreign policy. What role should it play? Even a good many members who supported the President's Vietnam policy have become deeply concerned about these questions.

The Constitution posits three major roles for Congress—through its action with respect to legislation, through its powers of the purse, and through the Senate's action on treaties and nominations. An important part of the power struggle between Congress and the executive branch has to do with the kind of actions the executive can take in the absence of legislative authority, and with the type of international agreements the President can make without Senate approval. These are essentially arguments involving differing interpretations of the Constitution. They have waxed and waned since 1789, depending in part on who occupied the White House, and they will continue to do so because they are not susceptible to judicial settlement or to precise definition.

More important, and far more frustrating from the congressional point of view, are the subtler policy questions which, once decided by the executive branch, may lead to a treaty, to a recommendation for legislation, or to requests for appropriations, but which do not initially involve formal congressional participation. For example, the Foreign Assistance Act has always provided the President with wide latitude to initiate new aid programs or to waive conditions with respect to either new or old programs. Congress approved these provisions for flexibility in the Foreign Assistance Act in response to the argument that new and unforeseen conditions could arise at any time in any part of the world. Yet so much have congressional attitudes changed in recent years that when such conditions do arise—in Cambodia in 1970, for example—a tremor runs through Congress when the President uses the powers given him, in this case, to supply military assistance to the Lon Nol government. Various members of Congress also get jittery, for completely opposite reasons, over diplomatic negotiations such as those involved in the strategic arms limitation talks (SALT) or in the never-ending Middle East crisis. Such negotiations could result in far-reaching American commitments which Congress may be called upon to ratify or support in one way or another in circumstances in which its freedom of action will be limited by the factual situation.

There are also congressional concerns that the executive branch may be involving the United States in foreign entanglements in a hundred different ways, or may even be committing it to policies, programs or courses of action without full and mature consideration by Congress. Some examples that suggest themselves are the arrangements our government makes for its military bases abroad, those under which it deploys nuclear weapons in other countries, or those by which it induces one country or another to support American policies in South Vietnam.

Finally, there are the frustrations arising from the larger questions of war and peace, questions which have to be decided for good or ill in a short time span and on the basis of secret information kept from the public. The Cuban missile crisis is a classic example. In critical situations such as this, there may be ways to achieve more meaningful congressional participation, but they have not yet been put into practice.

The fact that these questions frustrate Congress—or at least a significant part of its membership—is explicable mainly in terms of the alienation which has occurred between Congress and the executive branch in recent years. It is popularly known as the credibility gap, which is just another way of saying that a pervasive lack of trust has developed between the two branches of government. It will be remedied only when trust is restored, and while the restoration of trust would by no means guarantee a new consensus on fundamentals, it certainly would help. The nature of American politics is such that this new consensus, when developed, must embrace not only the two ends of Pennsylvania Avenue but the American people as well.

Congress and the Public

In the meantime, Congress finds itself caught in a sort of no-man's land between the executive branch and the public. Most discussion of congressional participation in the process of making foreign policy centers on its relationship with the executive branch, and this is indeed the dominant factor. But public opinion also participates on a continuing basis, and Congress has a vital relationship to the public as well as to the executive branch. The two relationships are, of course, strikingly different.

With respect to the public, Congress is usually concerned with questions of policy so broad and general that they might better be described as attitudes or opinions, while the relationship with the executive is more likely to be concerned with specifics. The legislative process itself is designed to deal with specifics and to pose questions which are decided by votes of yea or nay.

Should President Nixon's proposal to extend the ABM system be approved or not? Should the Non-Proliferation Treaty be accepted or rejected? Should the United States lift the limitations which it has imposed on trade with the countries of Eastern Europe? Should the foreign aid program be approved? If so, how much money should be appropriated for it? These are the kinds of questions which constantly confront the Congress and which normally call for a specific response.

As a part of its relationship with the executive branch, on the one hand, and with the public on the other, Congress performs the very useful function as a link between the two. This is the most difficult aspect of its participation in foreign policy to describe because it is so nebulous that one can hardly ever with certainty separate cause and effect. The fact is, however, that politicians, precisely because they are in close touch with local sentiment and are constantly evaluating the changing currents of public opinion, make an indispensable contribution to the policy process. Call it intuition, call it horse sense, call it sound political judgment—legislators are invaluable in helping to strike a tolerable balance between the idealistic and the practical, between the views of the expert and those of the general public. They help bridge an otherwise unbridgeable gap in the formation of our foreign policy.

The executive branch also has a direct relationship with the public. In periods such as the present when there are serious differences between Congress and the executive, a highly important aspect of the problem is the battle for public opinion. In this, the executive branch has a distinct advantage, because it is normally able to speak with one voice while Congress and the public clearly cannot.

The executive branch is, however, by no means monolithic. It consists of the many people who work for the federal government or who serve in its armed forces. Even the minute fraction of those who are involved in matters of high policy have differing points of view, and there are frequent clashes between the bureaucratic or institutional interests of the various departments, or between various parts within the same department. Certainly those who have helped in the formulation of our disarmament policies, for example, are well aware of the heated debates that have shaken the U. S. bureaucracy since 1945. But the point is the executive branch carries on its policy debates in private (or it tries to anyway), and in the end they are decided not by votes but by one man—the President.

When this point in the policy process has been reached, strenuous efforts are made within the executive branch to present a united front, and it is rarely that any serious cracks appear. The executive branch typically is loath to discuss a policy problem publicly until it has made up its mind as to the precise policy to be followed. Thereafter, the chances of Congress or any other outside source significantly affecting or altering the policy are very slim indeed. There are two major exceptions to this general statement, and they arise in connection with policies which require legislation (including appropriations) or treaties. Congress can, of course, amend legislation, and the Senate can put understandings or reservations on treaties, or legislation and treaties can be rejected entirely. But the executive branch typically fights tooth and nail against significant changes.

Furthermore, the President, simply by virtue of his office, has available enormously potent weapons to influence both Congress and the public. He has the vast resources of the executive branch at his beck and call. He lives in a glare of publicity which he can manipulate (the word is not used pejoratively) to his own ends. He and his advisers have debated in private; Congress and the people must carry on their debate in public.

One further aspect of the congressional role in foreign policy should be mentioned, namely, that Congress is a good deal more innovative in foreign policy than it is usually given credit for. Although many ideas have mixed parentage, some of the most imaginative and constructive foreign policies since World War II have originated in Congress. These include, to cite but a few leading examples, the exchange-of-persons program, the use of surplus agricultural commodities in the foreign aid program, the International Development Association, the Peace Corps, and the Arms Control and Disarmament Agency. Not infrequently an idea is born on Capitol Hill and then, when it is brought to fruition, the President receives political credit for it.

Partisan Politics

It must be emphasized that congressional participation in foreign policy probably has much less to do with partisan politics than most people realize. The two major party organizations occasionally issue pronouncements on foreign affairs, and the quadrennial party platforms always contain carefully prepared planks on foreign policy, but these are typically masterpieces of ambiguity and nobody, least of all the candidates, takes them very seriously. Each of the two major parties, in fact, is itself very often in wild disarray over foreign policy. Seldom is there a simple division between them on major international questions. Hawks, doves, and even mockingbirds abound in each, but there seems to be a general shortage of owls.

Some members of Congress, who belong to the same political party as the President, sometimes vote in favor of executive branch positions out of party loyalty, or simply because they are disposed to give the President the benefit of the doubt. The reverse is rarely true. Indeed, staff members on Capitol Hill can recall few if any instances in which a member of Congress belonging to the opposite political party from the President voted against an executive position on an important foreign policy question for purely partisan reasons. Politics may not always stop at the water's edge, but it usually does not venture very far beyond the three-mile limit.

It is significant that the opposition to the foreign policies of both Presidents Johnson and Nixon has embraced both Democrats and Republicans. The current deterioration in executive-legislative relations began in the Johnson administration with Democrats in control of both houses of Congress. A good many of Johnson's severest critics were good Democrats; some of Nixon's are good Republicans.

We are dealing here with honest differences of opinion as to what is best for the country in a changing world. These differences manifest themselves in the institutional relationships between the executive and the legislative branches of the government more than they do in the relationships between the two parties.

This ideological overlap makes it far more difficult for the differences to be worked out. The way the American system of government provides for resolving basic differences is through elections. But elections are fought along party lines and at regular intervals. Our two-party system, whatever its merits, does not readily provide a means for settling institutional differences which may arise from time to time outside the framework of party politics.

Yet the gulf between the Senate and the President which developed over the war in Vietnam has broadened to include basic differences over the proper constitutional roles and prerogatives of each. In some respects this is a much more fundamental issue even than the war. It is, of course, not a new one, having arisen at various times and in various forms throughout our nation's history.

Relations with the Executive Branch

The relationship of Congress with the executive branch lies at the heart of its role in foreign policy. Whatever that role is or should be, it has to be exercised in conjunction with the executive branch, whether in cooperation or conflict, whether independently or submissively. As the congressional role expands, the executive role tends to contract, and vice versa. Institutional jealousies being what they are, this naturally leads to friction and distrust, particularly at times when one or the other branch of the government is being more than usually self-assertive.

The American system of government is such that executive-legislative relationships tend to be negative and often of an adversary nature. Either branch can frustrate the other, but it is very difficult for either to control the other. The President, as our chief spokesman abroad, can negotiate a treaty, but he certainly cannot compel the Senate to give its advice and consent to ratification. The Senate can pass a resolution advising the President to make a treaty, but it cannot compel him to do so. The President can ask Congress for authority or funds to carry out a given program, but he cannot compel Congress to provide them. The Congress can give the President authority or funds which he has not requested, but it cannot compel him to use them.

A good deal of the executive-legislative relationship revolves around maneuvering on the part of the President or the Congress to avoid the potential for impasse or delay built into these respective constitutional powers. This is at least a part of the explanation for increased use of executive agreements, which can be concluded by the President on his own authority, instead of formal treaties. It also explains why Congress often earmarks money—i.e., provides that certain sums can be spent only for stated purposes. This does not insure that the funds in question will be spent in that way, but it does insure that if they are not spent for the specified purposes, they will not be spent at all.

As a consequence of these built-in constitutional relationships, a great deal of emphasis has traditionally been put on the need for executive-legislative cooperation. Indeed, if there is not a minimum of such cooperation, the government would approach a state of paralysis. This is perhaps what the framers of the Constitution intended. They were clearly more concerned with avoiding errors of commission than errors of omission. Their negative approach was in part a result of sad experience with English kings and unbridled governmental authority, but it was also based on the theory that doing nothing is less likely to have seriously adverse consequences than taking positive action and doing the wrong thing. The theory is especially applicable when a given course of action does not have widespread public support—when it does not, in other words, grow out of a general consensus.

Clearly, these considerations are more important in foreign policy than in domestic affairs. A case in point is the rather stiff constitutional requirement of a two-thirds vote in the Senate for the approval of treaties. The theory is that if a foreign policy cannot command that much support in the Senate, it is not a viable policy for the long run whatever its other merits might be. There is still much to be said for the theory, which explains many of the present difficulties faced by those responsible for the conduct of foreign policy. Some of these difficulties stem from the fact that rather than justify certain actions in public, the executive branch has found ways of taking them in secret. It found it far easier, for example, to obtain appropriations for the Central Intelligence Agency to subsidize the National Student Association secretly than for the Office of Education or the Department of State to do so openly. Congress, of course, shares complicity in the arrangement. It may validly be argued that most of the Congress did not know what it was doing, but this does not excuse the fact that most of the Congress did not insist on knowing.

The executive-legislative cooperation which is necessary for an effective foreign policy is naturally viewed from different perspectives at the two ends of Pennsylvania Avenue. From the point of view of the executive branch, in the baldest terms, it means congressional approval of the executive's proposals, policies, and actions. From the congressional point of view, it means serious consultation. In the trenchant phrase of Senator Arthur Vandenberg, if Congress is going to be in on the crash landings, it has to be in on the take-offs as well. The question of what constitutes meaningful consultation will be explored later. Suffice it to say here that the problem has become more acute as the result of two factors. One of these is that some of the most crucial foreign policy decisions have to be made in a hurry. The other is that from the executive point of view, Congress has sometimes approved a take-off and then changed its mind at the time of the crash landing. President Johnson frequently cited the 1964 Gulf of Tonkin resolution as a case in point. The reply to this charge, from the congressional side, is that Congress approved this particular take-off under a misapprehension—or, if we may continue the aviation analogy, that the pilot did not tell the co-pilot that the weather report was bad, that the fuel supply was low, or that the engines were not powerful enough for the plane and its cargo.

Quite apart from these traditional concepts of cooperation, there is yet another view that merits consideration. As some read the Constitution, it envisions a relationship of arm's length independence. This view, which has been gaining adherents, especially in the Senate, suggests that Congress ought to proceed independently of the executive branch, to consider foreign policy problems and arrive at its own judgment about them. Whether or not Congress reaches the same conclusion as the executive branch is purely coincidental and really ought not to be couched in terms of support for, or opposition to, the President. Given the way the media present the news, with the emphasis on conflict, this seems a rather purist and unrealistic attitude. But if Congress did behave this way, and did reach the same conclusion as the executive, the resulting policy would certainly rest on a much stronger base. And if Congress did not reach the same conclusion, this fact in itself should be enough to hoist storm warnings that the particular policy ought to be carefully re-examined.

If this view of the congressional role in foreign policy prevails, it has a good many implications as to how Congress organizes and equips itself to play the role. These matters will be examined later. For the moment, we are concerned with more fundamental questions. Whatever executive-legislative cooperation may mean, there are two ingredients which are indispensable for a viable policy for the long run. In the order of their importance, these are mutual trust and consensus. As noted, these elements are inter-related but they do not overlap completely. It may be quite possible, for example, to rebuild a feeling of mutual trust without developing a national consensus. It will be some years, if it is possible at all, before this country can build again the kind of general consensus or agreement which existed on foreign policy questions in the period after World War II.

Neither mutual trust nor consensus exist in sufficient measure today, and the two primary questions are: Why don't they exist? How can they be restored?

Chapter II

The Deterioration in Executive-Legislative Relations

The answer to the question why mutual trust does not exist is to be found in a review of executive-legislative relations since 1965. That year opened with the inauguration of a president who had been elected by the largest popular majority in history and who brought to office with him majorities of 68 to 32 in the Senate and 294 to 140 (with one vacancy) in the House. As Senator and a great legislative engineer, Johnson had dominated that unruly body as no one else in his or perhaps any other time. Yet a little more than three years and two months after his triumphal inaugural parade down Pennsylvania Avenue, Johnson took himself out of the 1968 election campaign in a speech which for human drama ranks with Edward VIII's abdication. During this time he had suffered not a single serious legislative setback. On the contrary, he had pushed through Congress the most far-reaching domestic program since the days of Franklin Roosevelt. With respect to foreign policy, Congress was no more recalcitrant than was its wont. The President even survived the mid-term elections of 1966 with majorities of 64 to 36 in the Senate and 247 to 187 (with one vacancy) in the House. What happened, then, to bring about the dramatic change that took place in 1968?

The Foreign Relations Committee

The story must be told in terms of the Foreign Relations Committee of the Senate, which happened to be composed (in large part because of the arangements made by Lyndon Johnson as Majority Leader a decade before) of an extraordinary group of men who dominated much of the news on foreign policy and acquired an influence beyond their numbers. By the end of 1968, veteran observers of the Washington scene were agreed that never in their memories had executive-legislative relations been worse, but what they meant was that never in their memories had relations between the executive branch and the Foreign Relations Committee been worse. Many opinions continued to be reflected in Congress as a whole, and in the House especially there was a strong inclination to give the President the benefit of the doubt.

This is an appropriate point to inject a word of caution about generalizations with respect to executive-legislative relations or congressional opinion. It is exceedingly difficult to describe a "congressional" point of view. Congress is composed of 535 strong-minded individuals, among whom one can usually find somebody who subscribes to almost any point of view within the realm of rational American political discourse. The story of the deterioration of executive-legislative relations since 1965 is really the story of how skepticism sometimes transcends policy disagreements. Throughout the 1960s Congress became increasingly dyspeptic about the foreign aid program, which did not, however, seriously impair its relations with the executive. What did impair relations was the credibility gap, the growth of distrust on both sides. This is a serious thing in a democracy, and worth examining in some detail.

Although none of the protagonists was to realize it until later, it began on a dark night in early August 1964 when an American destroyer in the Gulf of Tonkin was fired upon (or the Navy thought it was fired upon) by North Vietnamese torpedo boats. Reinforcements were sent and the destroyer, accompanied by a second destroyer, continued on what was represented as its routine patrol. A further attack was reported, and on August 5 President Johnson requested a joint resolution from Congress declaring the United States to be prepared, "as the President determines, to take all necessary steps, including the use of armed force, to assist any member or protocol state of the Southeast Asia Collective Defense Treaty requesting assistance in defense of its freedom." Congress approved the resolution two days later by a landslide vote of 416–0 in the House and 88–2 in the Senate. The issue then remained relatively dormant for the next two or three years. We shall return to it at the proper chronological point in the narrative.

The Dominican Republic

Although the Gulf of Tonkin affair became in time the most important cause for the loss of trust, the credibility gap was first opened in the spring of 1965 before the Vietnam war became a serious issue in Congress. The initial seeds of executive-legislative distrust were sown by the United States intervention in the Dominican Republic in late April 1965.

That unfortunate land had suffered under the singularly malign dictatorship of Rafael Trujillo for roughly thirty years prior to his assassination in 1961. After an interregnum (during which the Kennedy administration threatened to intervene to prevent a counter-coup by Trujillo's heirs), elections were held at the end of 1962 from which Juan Bosch, a kind of Caribbean Hamlet, emerged victorious. To no one's great surprise, Bosch was overthrown by a military coup d'état in 1963.

In April 1965 a military revolt occurred in the Dominican Republic, which was obviously something different from the routine coup. It was an attempt by some of the younger, more liberal officers to restore Bosch to power. Bosch, then in exile in Puerto Rico, hesitated. The armed forces in the Dominican Republic were divided. Widespread public disorder broke out. Communists or suspected Communists began to take part.

In these circumstances President Johnson ordered U.S. Marines, who had been standing by in a naval task force, into the Dominican Republic to evacuate Americans and other foreign nationals. The incident took on unusual significance inasmuch as it was the first military intervention by the United States in a Latin American country since the effective application of the Good Neighbor policy in the 1930s. Yet within a week there were 21,000 American troops in the country, and their stated mission was not only to evacuate foreigners but to prevent a Communist take-over while at the same time maintaining impartiality in what amounted to a Dominican civil war. The fact that this was seen as a contradiction on Capitol Hill seemed lost on the administration, which in any event certainly could not look with pleasure on the possible appearance of another Castro in the Caribbean.

Congress watched all of this more or less passively while it was developing. There were leadership meetings at the White House and briefings of committees on Capitol Hill. But after about a month, as the American involvement was obviously growing and as press reports from correspondents on the scene were not in harmony with the State Department line in Washington, the Foreign Relations Committee began to have doubts. The doubts led to a committee investigation involving a review of the reports and intelligence available to the President at the time he made his decision to intervene. Secret hearings followed.

The committee as a whole came to no conclusion and issued no report; it was clearly divided as to the wisdom of American policy. But its chairman, Senator Fulbright, made a speech in the Senate in which he declared American policy in the affair was "characterized by a lack of candor" and went further to question the premises on which American intervention had taken place. He went out of his way to absolve the President of responsibility, placing the blame instead on the President's advisers. Fulbright sent a copy of his speech to Johnson in advance with a note saying he was making it in an effort to be helpful. This communication, which apparently was not received in the spirit in which it was ostensibly sent, marked a significant break between two men who had previously been close personal friends. Fulbright's Senate office walls are still, ironically, decorated with personal photos warmly inscribed from his friend Lyndon B. Johnson. In the traumatic days following the assassination of John F. Kennedy, it was Senator Fulbright's wife who did Lyndon Johnson's Christmas shopping for his wife and daughters. But after the Dominican Republic speech, when Johnson went to the hospital for a gall bladder operation, a Johnson staff member signed a *pro forma* acknowledgement to the personal note the President received from Fulbright. Whether the resultant pique was justified or not, the fact remains that the situation went from bad to worse.

The significance of the Dominican Republic affair lay not only in the break which it opened between two close friends and powerful leaders but also and more importantly in Fulbright's characterization of administration policy as lacking in candor. In justifying United States intervention in the first instance, the President had perhaps unwittingly overstated the public disorder existing in the Dominican Republic. He had referred to "some 1500 innocent people [who] were murdered and shot, and their heads cut off." [1] No evidence was ever produced to support this statement. The President also said that the American Ambassador to the Dominican Republic had telephoned the President from under his desk while bullets were flying about. The Ambassador later publicly denied this.[2]

Whatever one might have thought about the validity of the real justification for the Dominican intervention—i.e., the danger of a Communist take-over—the facts as unravelled by the Foreign Relations Committee nurtured seeds of senatorial doubt over the discrepancies in the administration's explanation of its public position on that as well as other issues.

1. Press conference of June 17, 1965. *Department of State Bulletin,* Vol. LIII, No. 1358 (July 5, 1965), p. 20.
2. Senate Foreign Relations Committee, Hearing on the Nomination of William Tapley Bennett, Jr. to be Ambassador to Portugal, May 3, 1966, pp. 28–29 (unpublished transcript).

The Vietnam War

By far the most important of these other issues was the war in Vietnam, which in less than three years between 1965 and 1968 became the most contentious and explosive issue of this generation. In the process, it produced a mood of skepticism and self-assertiveness in Congress that is likely to last for years and that, while the war lasts, will increase congressional power and influence at the expense of the President. Moreover, Vietnam has been the prime cause of congressional sentiment for a fundamental re-examination of America's role in the world, its national interests and national priorities.

The tempest grew from a tiny cloud on the horizon. To borrow again from Senator Vandenberg's analogy, Congress may have been in on the take-off, but it chose to bail out before the crash landing. Supporters of the Johnson administration's policy might argue that the crash landing occurred *because* Congress bailed out; that if it had maintained a solid front in support of the administration, the policy would have been successful. Indeed, one of the sources of the bitterness which characterized executive-legislative relations in the later Johnson years was the feeling on the part of some administration officials that Congress approved the policy initially and then abandoned it when the going got rough. The record certainly provides some support for this view. It also explains why the anti-war elements in Congress are so sensitive about new American "commitments."

Back in September 1948, as Communist forces were overrunning mainland China, Congress added $75 million, which the President had not requested, to the foreign aid bill for use in the "general area of China." In May of the following year the administration initiated programs of economic and military assistance to the Associated States of Indochina and to France with the objective of restoring stability in the area and, as Secretary of State Dean Acheson phrased it, "permitting these states to pursue their peaceful and democratic development." Over the next two years, through the end of fiscal year 1952, these programs totalled $292 million, of which $245 million was military and $47 million economic assistance. (By the end of fiscal 1970, the total in Vietnam alone had reached $6.3 billion.)

During the siege of Dien Bien Phu in the spring of 1954, high administration officials briefly considered direct military intervention to rescue the French, but these proposals were rejected by President Eisenhower and were never subjected to any formal consideration by Congress. The French defeat at Dien Bien Phu led to the Geneva Agreements of July 1954, which provided for French withdrawal from Indochina, neutral status for Laos and Cambodia, and the partition of Vietnam along the 17th parallel pending elections in two years. The United States acquiesced in, but did not sign, the agreements. Congress responded by a provision in the Mutual Security Act of 1954 declaring its "sense" that none of the aid funds for Indochina should "be used on behalf of governments which are committed by treaty to maintain Communist rule over any defined territory of Asia."

Congress put another provision in the same act favoring "the creation by the free peoples of the Far East and the Pacific of a joint organization, consistent with the Charter of the United Nations, to establish a program of self-help and mutual cooperation designed to develop their economic and social well-being, to safeguard basic rights and liberties and to protect their security and independence." This was an advance endorsement of the Southeast Asia Collective Defense Treaty and its organization (SEATO), a project long favored by Secretary Dulles and a likeminded group in Congress. It now came to fruition at a conference in Manila in September 1954. Besides Dulles, the treaty was signed for the United States by Senators H. Alexander Smith, a New Jersey Republican, and Mike Mansfield, a Montana Democrat.

The key provision of the treaty is Article IV(1): "Each Party recognizes that aggression by means of armed attack in the treaty area against any of the Parties or against any State or territory

which the Parties by unanimous agreement may hereafter desig-
nate, would endanger its own peace and safety, and agrees that
it will in that event act to meet the common danger in accordance
with its constitutional processes." Cambodia, Laos, and South
Vietnam were precluded from joining the treaty by the Geneva
Agreements, but they were unanimously designated as covered
for the purposes of Article IV by a separate protocol. The Senate
gave its advice and consent to the ratification of the treaty on
February 1, 1955, by a vote of 82 to 1.

The partition of Vietnam was followed by an influx of approximately one million refugees from North to South, a stepped-up
U.S. aid program, and a national referendum which deposed Bao
Dai as Emperor and installed Ngo Dinh Diem as President of
South Vietnam. Diem's immediate security problem was quelling
the insurgency of various dissident religious sects. Successful in
this effort, he was strongly supported by the United States government and by most of the members of Congress (notably including Senator Mansfield) who expressed any views on the matter.
In February 1955, the U.S. Military Assistance Advisory Group
(MAAG) took over the training of the South Vietnamese army,
following the relinquishing of command authority by the French.
In the four-year period, 1953–57, total U.S. assistance to Vietnam
amounted to $1.1 billion—$277.8 million in military aid and
$823.3 million in economic aid.

Toward the end of the 1950s Communist guerrilla activity in
South Vietnam increased in tempo, and in May 1960 the United
States announced that the strength of its MAAG would be aug-
mented from 327 to 685 by the end of the year. The early 1960s
were marked by steady deterioration—establishment of the National Front for the Liberation of South Vietnam (the Viet Cong),
growing opposition within South Vietnam to the Diem government (culminating in its overthrow in November 1963), increasing infiltration from North Vietnam, and increasing commitment
of United States military advisers from 800 in 1960 to 23,300 in
1964.

Growing Opposition in Congress

This enlarged commitment by the United States was viewed with growing misgivings in Congress. In September 1963, following a summer of political turmoil in South Vietnam, 32 Senators led by Frank Church of Idaho co-sponsored a resolution calling for discontinuance of aid to South Vietnam unless its government put needed reforms into effect. The resolution did not pass the Senate, but a milder version, leaving the matter to the discretion of the President, was included in the foreign aid bill. In its report on that bill, the Foreign Relations Committee commented that "if the political situation in South Vietnam deteriorates further to the detriment of the war effort, the committee will be disposed to give further consideration to the more drastic steps called for" by the resolution.[3]

This proved an empty threat, in part because of the overthrow of the Diem government, and in large part because the presidential election year of 1964 introduced a new and important element in the debate. Senator Barry Goldwater of Arizona, the Republican nominee, and his supporters called for stronger military action in Vietnam. President Johnson campaigned as a moderate, repeating that "we seek no wider war" and arguing against sending "American boys to do the job that Asian boys should do." In the face of Senator Goldwater's attacks, Democratic members of Congress who had serious doubts about the wisdom of U.S. involvement in Vietnam nonetheless supported the President.

These political attitudes partly explain the rapid, overwhelming approval that Congress gave to the Southeast Asia resolution following reported attacks by North Vietnamese torpedo boats on the U.S. destroyers *Maddox* and *C. Turner Joy* in the Gulf of Tonkin in August 1964. The United States responded with air strikes against the North Vietnamese torpedo boat bases, an action that appeared restrained in the circumstances. Yet Senator

3. Senate Foreign Relations Committee, Report on Foreign Assistance Act of 1963 (S. Rep. 588, 88th Cong. 1st Sess.), p. 8.

Fulbright, who managed the resolution in the Senate as chairman of the Foreign Relations Committee, was later to say that he regretted his role more than anything else he had ever done. Senator Mansfield, the Majority Leader, was to say some four years later that he would not have voted for the resolution if he had known in 1964 what he knew in 1968. In 1970, as if to clear a troubled conscience, the Senate voted not once but twice to repeal the Tonkin resolution with President Nixon's approval.

At least a part of what Mansfield had not known in 1964 was developed as the result of the Foreign Relations Committee's later meticulous review of the Gulf of Tonkin incident. The review was inspired in 1967 by several indications that the incident had not been accurately reported at the time it occurred. Analysis of the ships' logs and of Navy messages to and from the ships raised serious questions about the scope of the attacks (whether one in fact occurred at all) and whether they were provoked by the United States. The retaliatory air strikes, which had seemed moderate at the time, now appeared to some to be more extreme than the provocation warranted. In his last appearance before the Committee as Secretary of Defense, Robert McNamara stoutly defended the administration version; but he did not convince all the members of the Committee, and the credibility gap unfortunately widened.

The committee's review, however, was more than two years after congressional, particularly Senate, opposition to the administration's Vietnam policy had been made explicit by a group whose numbers continued to grow. The turning point had come in the President's press conference of July 28, 1965, when he announced an increase in U.S. troops in Vietnam from 75,000 to 125,000. (By the spring of 1968, they had increased to more than 500,000, including those in Thailand.) The sharp increase in the summer of 1965 led some Senators who had previously only questioned administration policy to take a stand against it. This trend was reinforced by the skepticism which the administration had brought on itself by its earlier extravagant statements about the Dominican Republic. Yet for a time, some of the privately doubting Senators showed extraordinary restraint in public—possibly in part out of deference to public opinion and in part to President Johnson's argument that a united front at home was an important key to success in Vietnam.

The opposition over Vietnam came into the open in February 1966 when the Foreign Relations Committee used an administration request for additional foreign aid for Vietnam as a vehicle for wide-ranging hearings on the basic policy issues involved. Senators Wayne Morse of Oregon and Ernest Gruening of Alaska, who had for a time been the only voices in the Senate clearly opposed to the Vietnam war, now found support from Fulbright, Clark, Church, Aiken, Cooper, McGovern and others.

The opposition did not spring full-blown from the initial hearings. It gathered momentum as time went by, as American casualties increased, as budgetary costs soared, and as popular resentment against the war continued to rise. Furthermore, Congress itself continued to be badly divided over the war. Throughout most of 1966 and 1967, some influential Senators were not only supporting the President's policies but urging him to take stronger action. Within a period of four days in January 1967, for example, Senator John Stennis of Mississippi, Chairman of the Preparedness Investigating Subcommittee of the Armed Services Committee, called for an intensification of the U.S. bombing of North Vietnam to include industrial and power installations and jet airfields, while Senator Fulbright called for a cessation of the air attacks against the North. As the Foreign Relations Committee provided a forum for opponents of the war, the Preparedness Subcommittee provided a forum for military leaders to urge stronger military action. On August 31, 1967, the subcommittee issued a report asserting that Secretary McNamara had "shackled" the bombing campaign and calling for the "closure, neutralization, or isolation" of the port of Haiphong.

In October 1967, Senator Mansfield suggested another approach to the United Nations. With 58 co-sponsors, he introduced a resolution urging the President to "consider taking the appropriate initiative . . . to assure that the United States resolution of

January 31, 1966, or any other resolution of equivalent purpose be brought before the Security Council for consideration." [4] The 1966 resolution had simply urged the Security Council to consider the situation in Vietnam. The Security Council had formally placed the matter on its agenda, but had never discussed it, partly because of the unwillingness of mainland China and North Vietnam to have anything to do with the United Nations.

In hearings before the Foreign Relations Committee, the Mansfield resolution was nevertheless supported by the administration as well as by a number of former U.S. delegates to the U.N. General Assembly and professors of international law. The committee approved it unanimously on November 16, and the Senate followed suit by a vote of 82 to 0 on November 30.

At the same time the committee acted on the Mansfield resolution it also approved another resolution, sponsored by Senator Fulbright, which expressed the sense of the Senate that the commitment of U.S. forces to future foreign wars should be in accordance with constitutional processes, "which, in addition to appropriate executive action, require affirmative action by Congress specifically intended to give rise to such commitment." [5] The Fulbright resolution was directly inspired by repeated administration references to the American "commitment" in Vietnam. Although worded in ambiguous generalities, its purpose was clear enough: to reassert the foreign policy prerogatives of Congress and to warn both the present and future administrations (as well as the rest of the world) not to take Congress for granted.

In the rush to adjourn Congress in 1967, the resolution was put off until 1968 when it was trapped behind a Senate filibuster over a civil rights bill. It was subsequently scheduled for Senate consideration the first week of April, but Fulbright and Mansfield agreed to a further postponement in the light of the President's dramatic speech of March 31 taking himself out of the 1968 presi-

4. S. Res. 180, 90th Congress. As with the 1966 resolution there was little chance the United Nations would take action, in part because of the continued U.S. bombings of North Vietnam.
5. S. Res. 151, 90th Congress.

dential campaign and limiting the bombing of North Vietnam. As the spring of 1968 passed into summer, other matters intervened—notably the Paris negotiations with North Vietnam and Senator Fulbright's re-election campaign which required his absence from Washington—and the resolution languished on the Senate calendar. It was, however, revived in 1969 and passed the Senate in June of that year by a vote of 70–16.

The President's March 31 speech and the subsequent negotiations in Paris took some of the heat out of the Vietnam issue in Congress, though it continued to loom large in the political campaigns of 1968.

The Nixon Administration

The Nixon administration took office in January 1969 pledged to end the war and with a widespread predisposition on Capitol Hill to give the new President the benefit of the doubt. In May, President Nixon announced the policy of Vietnamization: American troops would be withdrawn as South Vietnamese troops were trained and equipped to take over the fighting. This was followed in July by announcement of what later came to be known as the Nixon Doctrine: while keeping its treaty commitments, the United States would henceforth expect its Asian allies to assume the primary responsibility for providing the manpower for their own defense, with the United States providing a shield against nuclear threats and also furnishing military and economic assistance.

In pursuance of these policies, 110,000 troops were withdrawn from Vietnam by the spring of 1970, with an additional 150,000 scheduled to come out by the spring of 1971. Plans were also announced for the withdrawal of 20,000 from Korea out of a total of 60,000, and 6,000 out of 48,000 were also withdrawn from Thailand. Agreement in principle was reached with Japan for the reversion of Okinawa to Japanese administration, the details to be worked out by 1972. Finally, the long-stalled Paris peace negotiations were given at least a flicker of life in the late summer of 1970 with the arrival of veteran diplomat Ambassador David Bruce, the newly appointed chief American negotiator, and with the return to Paris of the other principals. This move was followed by a major new administration initiative in October proposing a cease-fire, an exchange of prisoners, and a broadening of the negotiations to include other interested countries. American casualties in Vietnam, which had been 14,591 killed in action in 1968, fell to 9,414 in 1969 and to 4,221 in 1970.

These developments were generally welcomed by Congress as reversing the trend toward ever-growing involvement, and beginning a trend toward winding down the war and withdrawing American forces from Vietnam. But congressional critics were not mollified to the extent the administration hoped. They saw Vietnamization as a policy designed to change the nature of the war rather than to end it, and they expressed concern over what they saw as the implication of the Nixon Doctrine that the United States might be called upon to fight wars by proxy through increased military and economic assistance to its allies.

Nevertheless, Nixon's policies succeeded in shifting the debate in Congress from American involvement in Vietnam to the pace at which that involvement was being reduced and the probability of a successful withdrawal within a reasonable period of time. In other words, the debate shifted from an issue with clear affirmative and negative sides to a less precise issue involving matters of degree. This change reduced the temperature on Capitol Hill somewhat, but not so much as the President's supporters had expected.

One reason the temperature remained fairly high stemmed from the larger debate that developed over American defense policy in general, in which the most important issue was the anti-ballistic missile (ABM). This larger debate, discussed in more detail later, was not directly related to Vietnam but was affected by it, particularly in that Vietnam had substantially increased congressional skepticism as well as its assertiveness.

The principal reason, however, was the sudden American-South Vietnamese move into Cambodia. That quaint land had long been used as a refuge by North Vietnamese and Viet Cong troops fighting in South Vietnam, and some important enemy supply lines ran through it. American and South Vietnamese military leaders had long chafed at the restrictions which prevented them from wiping out these sanctuaries. In March 1970, Prince Norodom Sihanouk, who had successfully walked the tight rope of neutrality ever since the Geneva Conference of 1954, was deposed. The government which succeeded him, composed in large part of his own advisers, took a more anti-Communist stance.

The question of American policy toward Cambodia at once arose in acute form. Although the Foreign Relations Committee never expressed itself as a collegiate body, the strong view of a large majority of its members was against any United States involvement there. At a meeting on April 27 with Secretary of State William P. Rogers, 10 out of 11 members of the committee present expressed themselves to this effect in unequivocal terms. During the meeting the discussion centered on the question of furnishing military equipment to Cambodia. Although Rogers was not asked any direct questions about the possibility of an American strike against the enemy sanctuaries in Cambodia, he apparently gave no clear hint that the government was contemplating any involvement of that kind. On the other hand, he did not deny the possibility. In any event, it was only three days later, on the night of April 30, that President Nixon announced the American military incursion into Cambodia.

If anything were needed to set the committee and the executive branch at loggerheads again, as in the late Johnson period, this was it. Members of the committee concluded either that Rogers had deceived them or that he himself had been deceived or kept uninformed by the White House and the Pentagon. Or was it possible he had withheld information in order to cover the secrecy of the operation? Each conclusion was equally distasteful. Members of the committee liked Rogers personally. Many had known him since his own days on Capitol Hill where he served with distinction as staff director of the Permanent Investigations Subcommittee in the late 1940s. Despite the element of personal friendship, and despite the good faith of the Secretary, the credibility gap widened further.

In the Senate it is a long-standing tradition that one may disagree strongly with a colleague on an important policy matter and still be his friend. In other words, friendly relations may create a more cordial atmosphere for the discussion of serious problems but they do not necessarily result in agreement. As James Reston of *The New York Times* has pointed out, Fulbright, Rogers, and Laird play golf together from time to time on the Burning Tree golf course and thus enjoy a sort of "shared misery." They may have improved their golf somewhat, but some deep foreign policy differences have remained unresolved.

Meanwhile, a spasm of protest convulsed the nation's college and university campuses, and tragic incidents like those at Kent and Jackson State added greatly to the emotional setting. Senators Cooper, a Republican, and Church, a Democrat, introduced an amendment to the foreign military sales bill then pending before the Foreign Relations Committee to forbid the use of funds to maintain American combat troops in Cambodia or other military activities in support of the Cambodian government. The committee adopted the amendment promptly, but debate in the Senate lasted over a period of seven weeks. In the course of the debate a proposal by Senator Byrd to declare that the President, as Commander-in-Chief, could retain troops in Cambodia if he thought it necessary to protect American lives in Vietnam was rejected by a vote of 47 to 52. Finally on June 30, the amendment, somewhat modified, was agreed to by a vote of 58 to 37. The bill was sent to a House-Senate conference committee which promptly deadlocked.

The Senate debate on the Cooper-Church amendment was followed shortly by debate on an amendment offered by Senators George McGovern (Democrat of South Dakota) and Mark Hatfield (Republican of Oregon) to the military procurement authorization bill, forbidding the use of funds to keep American troops in Vietnam after December 31, 1971. This amendment was finally rejected on September 1, 1970, by a vote of 39 to 55.

In these amendments, and in an earlier one put on the Defense Department appropriation bill in December 1969 prohibiting funds for American ground combat troops in Laos and Thailand, the Congress for the first time in the postwar period was seriously considering using its power of the purse to check the President's power as Commander-in-Chief. The administration accepted the restraint in the case of Laos and Thailand, making clear that it had no intention of sending ground combat troops there anyway. It strongly resisted the proposal in the cases of Cambodia and Vietnam, arguing that such a limitation would unduly restrict executive flexibility in coping with unforeseen contingencies. Possibly one reason the Senate heeded the administration's objections in the case of Vietnam but not in the case of Cambodia was that by the time it got around to voting on the Cooper-Church amendment, the last American troops were leaving Cambodia.

Evaluation of the Cambodian episode varied widely, depending on one's view of the Vietnam war, the Congress, and the Presidency. Thus, the *Washington Post* characterized the "no-more-Cambodias" vote on the Byrd proposal in the Senate on June 11 as an "historic occasion" and "an exhilarating bid for restoration of Congress to its historic and constitutional role." [6] On the other extreme, columnist William S. White denounced the entire debate as "the most absurd and fatuous scene of battle in the United States Senate within memory. . . ." The Cooper-Church proposal, he said, emerged "as the most explicit reaffirmation of the inherent powers of the commander-in-chief ever to issue from a legislative body, in war time or otherwise." [7]

Meanwhile, on both sides of the Capitol, many people had begun to think about ways of spelling out in law appropriate limits on the President's authority as Commander-in-Chief. In the House, this took the form of a joint resolution approved by the Foreign Affairs Committee in September 1970 requiring the President to submit a detailed report to Congress whenever he committed the armed forces to combat, or deployed them abroad

6. *Washington Post,* June 14, 1970.
7. *Ibid.,* July 4, 1970.

equipped for combat, or substantially enlarged their deployment in a foreign nation. In the Senate, it took the form of a bill, co-sponsored by the unusual combination of Senators Javits and Dole, which approached the problem somewhat differently. The Javits-Dole bill spelled out four circumstances in which the President, as Commander-in-Chief, could use the armed forces: to repulse a sudden attack against the United States; to repulse a sudden attack against its armed forces on the high seas or lawfully stationed abroad; to protect U.S. nationals abroad; and to comply with a national commitment in which Congress had participated. However, the bill went on to require affirmative congressional approval of such action within thirty days and to provide that, failing such approval, the action could not be sustained.

As the Ninety-first Congress drew to a close the Javits-Dole bill remained in the freezer largely because Congress was concerned with other more urgent matters. But the truce between the President and the Congress, if it could be called a truce, promised to be a temporary one. For the Ninety-first Congress, like the Ninetieth before it, had demonstrated a new mood on Capitol Hill; in the words of Senator Javits, its term marked the "beginning of a new assertiveness and a new activism by the Congress." And accompanying this mood was a strong determination to rectify the imbalance of power that had developed over the years between the executive and legislative branches of government.

Some informed observers in Washington, however, believed the balance had already shifted too far in the direction of Congress. As the *Washington Evening Star* put it, some of the more assertive members of the Senate are demanding a new role in foreign policy—"to advise and dissent." This means, in effect, that if the President rejects their advice on major policy issues "there will be considerable hell to pay. . . . Surely it is a fallacy," continued the *Star*, "that long and bitter debates—such as those over Vietnam or the ABM—result in better policy or greater national unity. . . . Controversy, of course, is essential to democracy. But what we are moving toward today is institutionalized dissension. If it is carried far enough, the country could, in fact, become ungovernable." [8]

Here, it seems to me, is the crux of the matter. If contacts between Congress and the President produce nothing but warm and cordial relations, then obviously Congress would be playing no useful role of its own. On the other hand, if they produced only conflict and strife, the government could not perform its normal functions. The task we face, in a separation-of-powers system, is to reach a reasonable compromise between the two extremes so that acceptable policies and programs can be forged from a maze of conflicting ideas and objectives.

In short, under our system of government the relationship between the President and the Congress is not supposed to be one of peace and harmony, of sweetness and light. On the contrary, it is a relationship in which friction, within proper limits, can be a creative factor; in which tension, up to a point, can be a positive element; in which jockeying for power, within reasonable bounds, is a normal development. But one of the characteristics of our government is that each branch can sabotage the other if it chooses to do so. It follows that a reasonable degree of cooperation and teamwork between the two branches is essential if our system is to function effectively in the interests of the nation.

Admittedly, this is a delicate balance to maintain. I would suggest, however, that while mutual trust and confidence are essential elements in our foreign policy, they should not be emphasized to the point where independence of judgment is forsaken and creativity and innovation in our system are sacrificed.

8. January 6, 1970.

Chapter III

The Future of Executive-Legislative Relations

We turn now to the question of how mutual trust and consensus can be restored. Given the depth of the breach in current executive-legislative relations, this could be a long time in coming. It is more likely to come through patient building on small areas of agreement than through re-ordering existing mechanisms or inventing new ones. The lack of trust is in part a by-product of the lack of consensus; and the wider the differences, the more time—and talk—is required to rebuild consensus. Mechanistic arrangements can help a good deal, but they are certainly not an end in themselves. Indeed, in the present atmosphere, almost any suggestion for reorganizing executive-legislative relations is likely to be viewed with suspicion by one side or the other.

Even in the era of close collaboration in the late 1940s, many students of the subject were preoccupied with essentially mechanistic devices to preserve and build upon the good relations that developed. The first Hoover Commission on the Organization of the Federal Government recommended creation of the position of Assistant Secretary of State for Congressional Relations, and that office in fact has become a vital channel of continuing communication. The notion has persisted, however, that if only ways could be found to bring Congress and the executive branch closer in terms of human contacts and sharing of information and problems, they would become closer also in their view of the way in which the problems should be solved.

Although the role of Congress in foreign policy is much too fundamental to be solved by new methods of communication, it is nonetheless worthwhile to search the gamut of executive-legislative relations to determine if there are any such devices which might ameliorate the current conflict or at least help to contain it. There are several, some of which have been tried with varying degrees of success and some of which are relatively new. They involve more intimate consultation with Congress, more information for Congress, and participation by members of Congress in the diplomatic process as advisers or as members of delegations to international conferences. Pervading all these relationships is a subtle culture gap between Congress and the bureaucracy that should also be explored.

Consultation with Congress

First let us examine the problem of consultation which lies at the very heart of executive-legislative relationships. It is without doubt the most important single factor in the development of satisfactory working relations for the formulation of American policy.

Consultation can be a success or failure, depending on the goodwill and determination of those who are trying to make it work. There are, of course, many examples of effective consultation in the postwar era. Secretary Cordell Hull's frequent meetings with eight members of the House and Senate prior to the San Francisco Conference in 1945, in order to secure executive-legislative cooperation in developing plans for the United Nations Charter, were a brilliant success and set a standard for the future. Executive branch relations with Capitol Hill were equally cordial during the evolution of the Marshall Plan when consultations with both the House and Senate were close and continuous. Still another flawless performance was turned in by John Foster Dulles who, as principal negotiator, frequently consulted with Senate leaders during the negotiations that led to the signing of the Japanese Peace Treaty in 1952.

One can cite a good many other examples, including a number of treaties, especially during the decade after World War II when Congress was heavily involved with the executive in laying the foundations for American participation in the postwar world. In more recent years this type of consultation has fallen off considerably, partly because there have been fewer important pieces of legislation and treaties for Congress to consider.

Probably the least important aspect of consultation is the technique that is used. Of greater moment are what those involved think the term means and the purposes which they think are being served by it. The idea of consultation is fine, the argument on the congressional side runs; the trouble is that all too often it has been sporadic, ill-timed, and inadequate. Or as one influential Republican member of the House Foreign Affairs Committee said to the writer in 1970: "They tell you only what they want to tell you. They don't tell you anything they don't want you to know."

In recent years criticisms of this kind, whether justified or not, have become more frequent—especially since the expansion of the Vietnam war. Typical, perhaps, is the comment by Senator Muskie who complained about the administration's failure to consult Congress prior to the incursion into Laos in February 1971. "We were not consulted," he said. "We were confronted with a *fait accompli* . . . and it is an outrage. . . . We were not given an opportunity to advise." [1]

To consult, in the eyes of the State Department and the White House, frequently means to inform. There is, of course, a big difference. The setting may run all the way from an informal telephone call to a congressional staff member to a solemn meeting of the congressional leadership with the President at the White House. But the script is usually much the same: this is the situation; this is what we are going to do about it. Members of Congress may comment if they desire, but only rarely are they in a position to change anything.

This approach naturally affects the purposes which the partici-

1. *U.S. News and World Report,* February 22, 1971.

pants think are being served. Rarely is the purpose, from the point of view of the executive branch, what the literal meaning of consultation would imply—that is, the seeking of some one's opinion and advice before any final decision is reached. More often the purpose is, at a minimum, to eliminate congressional criticism that comes from first learning of an action from the news media; or, at a maximum, to generate support, hopefully bipartisan, for a course of action already decided on. The process of consultation thus frequently degenerates into a meaningless charade.

The State Department's criteria of what to consult Congress about are almost as bizarre as the criteria Congress applies for determining its own priorities. In the spring of 1966, for example, the Department saw fit to distract the Senate Foreign Relations Committee over a minor point in a proposed treaty relating to tuna fishing in the South Atlantic, but later in the year it was willing to talk about the American military build-up in Thailand only after repeated prodding and then only in closed session. Further, as Senator Fulbright noted in a press conference, the Department took pains in advance to notify the committee of the nomination of an Ambassador to Senegal, but the committee learned through the press of the nomination of Nicholas Katzenbach to be Undersecretary of State.

One of the criticisms most often heard is that consultation is geared to periodic crises and not to long-range issues. In practice, it would seem to be based more on the idea of fire-fighting rather than on the more constructive concept of fire-prevention.

In June 1967, for example, *after* the smoldering Middle East crisis broke into open hostilities, there was a good deal of consultation between top officials in the executive branch and the foreign-policy committees of Congress. Every aspect of the crisis was examined in great detail. But in the four or five weeks *prior* to the outbreak of war—while tension between Israel and the Arab states steadily mounted—little if any consultation took place. I am not arguing that in this particular instance congressional advice might have prevented disaster. But I would argue that Congress cannot play its role on the fire-prevention side if it is not made a part of the fire-prevention team.

It must be recognized, however, that true consultation is extraordinarily difficult, if not impossible, to carry out with respect to those problems that are characterized by the need to decide quickly or secretly, or both. And these are among the most important problems that the people charged with the conduct of foreign policy have to face.

Take, for example, the introduction of Soviet missiles into Cuba in 1962. The initial intelligence showing the presence of the missiles came from sources that were, at the time, secret—although Senator Kenneth Keating of New York apparently had access to much of the information. Aside from this, it would have been highly inadvisable, for a number of reasons, to make the intelligence public without concurrently announcing what the United States proposed to do about it. Even within the executive, extraordinary precautions were taken to restrict the intelligence and consideration of the problem to a very small group. Subsequent accounts by members of this group, notably Attorney General Robert F. Kennedy and Presidential Counsel Theodore Sorensen,[2] make it clear that prolonged consideration changed the conclusions which were reached.

In the circumstances, after the decision on what to do had been made, leading members of Congress were summoned to the White House to be told—approximately two hours before the whole world was told. President Kennedy and his advisers were disappointed and somewhat irritated by the congressional reaction, mainly because the members of Congress did not immediately reach the same conclusion the President and his advisers had reached after a week of intensive consideration. As President Kennedy remarked later to Sorensen, "My feeling is that if they had gone through the five-day period we had gone through—in

2. Robert F. Kennedy, *Thirteen Days* (New York: W. W. Norton & Co., 1969). Theodore C. Sorensen, *Kennedy* (New York: Harper & Row, 1965).

looking at the various alternatives, advantages and disadvantages . . . they would have come out the same way that we did." [3]

This is the crux of the matter. A member of Congress who is suddenly confronted with an unexpected and complex situation can hardly be expected to react initially as he would react after thinking about it for several days.

Nor is time the only consideration. Other important factors have to do with the *frequency* of consultation and the *amount* of information available. Someone has put the dilemma that often faces the executive branch in these terms: "If you tell the Congress too much they go crazy; if you don't tell them enough they go fishing." Somewhere between these two extremes is a golden mean—which has to be searched out in each case—based upon the importance of the subject matter, the desirability of congressional involvement, and the need to know.

President Johnson informed members of Congress of the decision to intervene in the Dominican Republic after the order had been given and before it became public knowledge. From all accounts, no serious questions were raised at that time, though many were raised later. Given the information gap between the President and the Congress with respect to the Dominican situation, it is difficult to see how the procedure could have been otherwise. The President and his advisers had been subjected to a constant stream of reports from Santo Domingo for several days. The President said he was sending Marines to evacuate U.S. citizens and other foreign nationals. The intervention turned out to involve a good deal more than that, but how was an outsider to know?

In situations like the missile crisis and possibly even the Dominican intervention it is difficult to have timely and meaningful consultation within the present framework of executive-legislative relations. Where there is a need for great secrecy in the decision-making process, the question at once arises as to which of the 535 members of Congress are to be consulted. It may introduce

3. Sorensen, cited, p. 702.

thorny issues of seniority and party politics but it is, by no means, an insuperable obstacle.

In the process of deciding to launch the Bay of Pigs operation, President Kennedy consulted Senator Fulbright, more by chance than by design. The Senator gave his views, which were quite negative; they were considered by the President and rejected. By the same formula, it would have been possible in the missile crisis for the President to have called in one or two Senators at the beginning, and they could then have gone through the process that the officials of the executive branch went through. This assumes that the Senators would have been able and willing to devote equal time to the process. It is not always a safe assumption, even in a case of such transcendent importance as the missile crisis, especially when the Senators were in the last weeks of a political campaign, as was the case at that time.

Furthermore, one or two Senators—or even the congressional leadership—can scarcely speak for Congress. Purists would argue that true consultation can take place only if the President lays the problem formally before Congress in a presidential message with or without recommendations and then awaits the outcome of congressional debate and action. Such a course is obviously impractical in critical ventures such as the Bay of Pigs, and is undesirable in cases such as the missile crisis. In the latter instance, if the President had called Congress into special session and revealed the presence of Soviet missiles in Cuba, he might well have encountered a very belligerent mood, making it difficult indeed to come out of the crisis without going to war.

The case of the Dominican Republic is somewhat different. Given the situation which existed at the time—that is, extreme disorder and a presumed physical threat to American nationals and other foreigners there—the President might have received prompt congressional support for a limited intervention to evacuate them. Whether he would have received support for the more extensive intervention which occurred is problematical, but it seems unlikely, at least in the same time-frame in which the intervention took place. It can be argued that timing was of the essence, but it is hard to see how this factor would apply beyond the evacuation of foreigners in the Dominican Republic unless one assumes also that the United States had a right and possibly even a duty to end the civil war. And this question in itself would be a proper subject for consultation. Obviously, one of the main reasons for intervention was to prevent the success of the revolution, a success which would have brought in its wake, so the administration feared, an unacceptable risk of a Communist government in the Dominican Republic. Whatever one may think about that, it is clear that the United States had the power to intervene later as well as earlier, though it must be admitted that the political liabilities would no doubt have been increasingly greater with the passage of time.

Thus in the case of the missile crisis, reference of the matter to Congress might well have produced a more explosive reaction than the adminitsration desired, while reference of the Dominican situation to Congress might well have produced delay or even no action at all. Views about what the executive-legislative relationship *should* have been in these matters are inevitably colored by the outcome.

An illuminating footnote is that following the missile crisis, Secretary of State Dean Rusk urged the Foreign Relations Committee to investigate the executive branch's handling of the affair, but the committee turned a deaf ear to this suggestion. Following the Dominican intervention, the committee on its own initiative conducted a meticulous and generally critical investigation.

Cynics might conclude that the executive branch can draw the moral that nothing succeeds like success. This judgment is reinforced by the fact that so far as the Dominican Republic itself is concerned, the situation there developed much better, at least in the short term, than the critics had predicted. No doubt the critics would answer by saying that the results are not yet in with respect to the long-term polarization of Dominican society. Nor are the results in with respect to the secondary effects of the Dominican intervention in other Latin American countries, particularly in terms of strengthening the resistance of oligarchies to change through implanting the idea that *in extremis* the United States will save them from any revolution with the taint of communism.

If consultation is going to contribute to the restoration of mutual trust and the building of a consensus, it has to take place in more of a give-and-take framework and with better informed members of Congress. In cases in which time is not of the essence and the issue is a broad and general one—for example, what to do about the foreign aid program or U.S. trade policy—the existing organizational arrangements work reasonably well. In cases of more immediate concern, it might be useful to consider (as suggested in a later chapter) the possibility of inviting some of the leaders of Congress to sit in on the deliberations of the National Security Council.

Although members of the House and Senate frequently charge the executive branch with failure to consult, this may well be a case of the pot and the kettle, for often a good share of the blame lies with Congress. Consultation is, after all, a two-way street. In point of fact, State Department officials ordinarily stand ready to consult about a good many problems, but they sometimes find it difficult, if not impossible, to round up an attentive audience on Capitol Hill. The day-to-day pressure on Congress is so great that many members are reluctant to consult about anything less than burning problems which have begun to hit the front pages of the daily press. Yet it should be obvious that consultation must take place before the headline stage if congressional ideas are to have real utility in the policy-making process.

As a general operating principle, it seems to me that our government should assure the most effective consultation possible on all important issues at all times—subject of course, to the overriding need for complete secrecy in certain cases. One comes back in the final analysis, however, to the hard fact that no amount of consultation can substitute for the processes of congressional debate, followed by approval, disapproval, or amendment. What consultation can do—and this is a great deal—is to lead to a meeting of the minds between the executive branch and selected congressional leaders. It can also be instrumental in developing helpful patterns of cooperation between the two branches. But it does not necessarily commit the Congress as a whole, and even less does it answer the question as to which executive actions require formal congressional approval.

Senator George Aiken of Vermont, in a Senate speech on November 24, 1970, emphasized the fact that adequate consultation remains the key to the restoration of sound legislative-executive relations. Consultation over Vietnam really ended in 1965, he pointed out, and the great escalation of the war started "without consultation with the Senate." It was in part this suspension that led him "to publicly disagree" on Vietnam. "If there is discontent in the Senate over the conduct of foreign policy," the Senator concluded, "it is because President Nixon has not yet restored the habit of consultation that lapsed during earlier years."

More Adequate Information

Whatever system of consultation exists, adequate information for Congress is crucial to the process. And in this, the willing cooperation of the executive branch is indispensable, for much of the information can only be supplied by the executive. It includes some (though by no means all) intelligence, the government's own raw reporting, and most important, perhaps, the executive's own records of its dealings with foreign governments.

Intelligence was crucial to the policy-making process in both the Cuban missile crisis and the Dominican intervention. In the former case, the intelligence was clear and unambiguous; in the latter, almost everything depended on how it was interpreted. What was initially given to Congress and the public was the administration's interpretation of the intelligence. It was not until the press and Congress examined what lay behind this interpretation that it appeared to some critics to be exaggerated and unjustified.

The government's own raw reporting was crucial in the Gulf

of Tonkin case—in this instance, the Navy messages to and from the ships involved. Meticulous reconstruction of the Tonkin incident, based on these messages and on the ships' logs, revealed a substantially different set of circumstances and sequence of events than had been presented to Congress and the public at the time.

The United States government's own records of its dealings with foreign governments have revealed, in some cases, a network of commitments and involvements which go beyond what many members of Congress thought would be involved when they approved the treaties and legislation underlying the commitments. These include many notes, plans, memoranda, agreements, understandings, etc., which greatly extend the formal provisions of the treaties that are the foundation for SEATO and NATO, for example.

Prime examples of these expanded commitments are the understandings with the Philippines, Korea, and Thailand about the allowances and other special benefits which the United States paid for Filipino, Korean, and Thai contingents in Vietnam; Air Force activities over Laos; military contingency planning with Thailand; and terms of agreements concerning the deployment of nuclear weapons in various NATO countries. These matters, of course, are quite apart from the political implications stemming from the physical and visible presence of American troops and the impact of large-scale military assistance programs.

All of these factors necessarily affect the parameters within which American foreign policy is made and American diplomacy is conducted. If Congress is to act intelligently on such legislation as foreign aid, military assistance, and appropriations, it needs to know about them. Yet, largely because of the secrecy factor, Congress often encounters great resistance in the executive branch in gaining access to the facts, and even more resistance in persuading the executive to make them public.

The executive branch has also traditionally been reluctant to give Congress access to its policy-planning documents at an early enough stage to be significant. The argument is that such documents are internal working papers and have no standing until approved by the Secretary of State, or the National Security Council, or whoever is responsible. The result is virtually to deny Congress effective access to the policy-making process until it has been completed. This is particularly irritating when a given executive branch study may be circulated privately to a number of consultants outside the government at the very time it is being denied to Congress. It should be pointed out, however, in fairness to the executive position, that outside consultants are under strict obligation not to reveal the contents of such studies while members of Congress are not.

This executive branch attitude is further reflected in two positions, one of which is valid, the other not. The valid position is that the President, the Secretary of State, and other officials are entitled to have confidential conversations and to receive confidential advice from their subordinates. It is a legitimate privilege, with which no one quarrels. Indeed, Congress claims a kind of legislative privilege of its own: some committees will not make available transcripts of their executive sessions. But it is stretching executive privilege a bit by applying it to a report prepared by an inter-agency committee which might have involved dozens of people one way or another. There is nothing very confidential about that.

The invalid source of executive concern lies in the use Congress might make of a planning document. Part of the fear stems from the traumatic experience of the McCarthy era when careers were ruined by demagogic and irresponsible attacks on Foreign Service officers because of the content of supposedly confidential memoranda. Another, and less defensible concern flows from a desire of the executive branch to make up its mind by itself, and from a reluctance to open the policy-making process to congressional participation for fear Congress might urge a different conclusion or course of action.

The McCarthy-type fear, while understandable, is really irrelevant to the aspect of the problem discussed here. The legitimate congressional interest lies in the ideas contained in planning documents; Congress is interested only incidentally, if at all, in the identity of the individuals who produced the ideas. This does not, of course, preclude the possibility of another McCarthy. But the possibility of a McCarthy appearing on the scene ought not to cut Congress off from meaningful participation in policy-making at an early stage.

Another explanation of why the executive branch resists giving Congress planning documents is the fear that individual members of Congress, for good reasons or bad, will seize certain recommendations and make an issue of them, even though they have not been approved and may, indeed, stand no practical chance of being approved.

Finally, there is the important point about security—that Congress, especially in recent years, is not to be trusted with sensitive or delicate information. This is where Congress is most vulnerable. And admittedly it is not a very convincing argument to insist, as some members do, that it is difficult to remember whether they obtained certain information from the press or from confidential government sources.

All of these arguments would be more persuasive if the executive branch were monolithic and leak-proof itself. But arguments have an interesting way of spilling out in public, not in an orderly manner, but piecemeal through leaks to the press or even to sympathetic members of Congress. Besides irritating Congress, it is hard to see what is accomplished by not supplying the documents Congress wants and needs—assuming, of course, that adequate arrangements are made for their security. This should not prove an impossible task, for Congress as a whole should have a keen interest in protecting its major source of classified information.

Congressional Participation in Diplomacy

Ever since the San Francisco Conference, which wrote the U.N. Charter in 1945, successive administrations have followed the practice of including members of Congress on delegations to international conferences. With the exception of the 1947–49 meetings, they have traditionally served on delegations to the U.N. General Assembly. According to an informal understanding between the executive and legislative branches, two members of the House are appointed in odd-numbered years (when there is no election) and two members of the Senate who are not up for re-election are appointed in even-numbered years. Members of Congress also frequently serve as advisers or observers at other international conferences, although there is no pattern for this kind of participation.

Generally speaking, the practice is beneficial for all concerned, though whether it is sufficiently beneficial to justify the time and effort involved is a closer question. Much depends upon the importance of the conference and whether the member of Congress takes his attendance seriously or whether he regards it primarily as a junket. A good deal depends also on the attitude of the executive branch delegation: Does it appreciate the presence of the member of Congress and expose him as much as possible to the substantive work of the conference, or does it view his presence as a potential nuisance and seek simply to divert him with visits to Peace Corps operations, AID housing projects, national museums, and the like?

A good deal depends also on the intrinsic importance of the conference and on whether it is expected to produce a treaty or other agreement which will require Senate approval or some other form of legislative action.

Inasmuch as the United States takes part in hundreds of conferences every year, the range of opportunities for congressional participation is very wide indeed. After World War II, Senators Tom Connally and Arthur Vandenberg sat through more than 200 meetings with Secretary of State James F. Byrnes in the negotiations that led to the signing of the peace treaties with Italy and the satellite states in 1947. At the other extreme is the story of a leading Senator who accepted an invitation to serve on the U.S. delegation to the World Health Assembly in Geneva. He stayed just long enough to have his picture taken with the

Director-General of the WHO and the President of the Assembly and then left for more interesting parts.

Leaving aside the General Assembly as a special case, congressional leadership, at least in the Senate, has tended in recent years to discourage attendance at international conferences. The reason has been purely pragmatic—congressional sessions are growing longer, and the leadership does not like to have any more Senators than absolutely necessary away from Washington when the Senate is in session.

The administration has likewise become somewhat erratic in its selection of conferences to which congressional representation is invited. Routine invitations go forth for such meetings as the Board of Governors of the Inter-American Development Bank or the World Health Organization. But no response is made to strong suggestions from the Foreign Relations Committee that one or more Senators should attend, at least sporadically, the SALT talks on limiting strategic arms. Congressional advisers are regularly invited to ministerial meetings of the Organization of American States, but not to ministerial meetings of NATO or SEATO, and the executive branch has been unwilling to give the Foreign Relations Committee the same briefings on nuclear weapons policy that it gives the NATO defense ministers. The Inter-American Development Bank, the WHO, and the OAS are all estimable institutions and serve very useful purposes, but their impact on world affairs is hardly to be compared with what happens at NATO or SALT.

It is, of course, impractical to expect a Senator to spend months (especially while the Senate is in session) observing, or even actively participating in, tedious arms control negotiations in Vienna or Helsinki. However, during the equally tedious negotiations which resulted in the Nuclear Test-Ban and Non-Proliferation Treaties, a few interested Senators did keep in touch through occasionally visiting Geneva for a few days. It is a measure of the deterioration in executive-legislative relations that it was only after some argument from Capitol Hill that the White

House permitted the Director of the Arms Control and Disarmament Agency, Gerard C. Smith, to brief the Foreign Relations Committee on the SALT discussions in 1970.

This deterioration in relations probably explains the recent reluctance of the executive to invite congressional participation in really important international conferences. It might well fear that congressional participants would not be "team" players, that they might speak out of turn and create embarrassing diplomatic problems.

The other side of the coin is the degree to which a legislator's independence might possibly be compromised by attendance at a conference. Two different levels are involved here. With respect to a few conferences (the U.N. General Assembly is the most conspicuous example), congressional participants are full-fledged delegates—i.e., representatives, in the technical sense, of the United States government and subject to written instructions from the Secretary of State and the President. In effect, this means that delegates may be called upon to wear two hats; first as a maker of foreign policy and later as a possible critic of the policy he has helped to create. This obviously sets up a potential conflict, and it is a question which has troubled some members of Congress who have had both strong views and strong consciences. Historically, however, it has been no more than a potential conflict. Perhaps the nearest it came to materializing was in 1960 when Senator Wayne Morse of Oregon refused to cast the U.S. vote as instructed on a colonialism issue and turned the task over to a State Department official who happened to be with him at the time.

Other incidents of a more or less serious nature come to mind. Certainly Senator William F. Knowland's angry reference, in a General Assembly debate in 1956, to India's Krishna Menon as the "floor leader of the Soviet Union" did not improve relations between the United States and India. And clearly the insistence of some congressional delegates, during the 1950s especially, that they be permitted to play to the grandstand with tough speeches attacking the Soviet Union has not always been helpful to our posture in the United Nations. Incidents like these suggest that it would be less nerve-wracking for our professional diplomats if members of Congress were not invited as delegates to international conferences.

Most of the time, indeed, members of Congress participate in their capacity only as advisers or observers. Hence, their independence is compromised, if at all, only by the fact that by having participated in the process of negotiating a treaty or some other agreement which will require legislation, they may feel they have implicitly committed themselves to supporting it. In fact, there is an ancient suspicion on Capitol Hill, long antedating the current strains in executive-legislative relations, that any executive initiative for consultation is some kind of plot to commit Congress in advance and thereby limit its freedom of action. Strangely, although congressional distrust of the executive branch has grown markedly in recent years, this particular suspicion seems, if anything, to have diminished.

On balance, congressional participation in international conferences seems to have done very little harm and some good. In a few cases—the conferences leading up to the peace treaties with the satellite states, or the San Francisco conference on the U.N. Charter—congressional cooperation has been of inestimable value, not only in the drafting process but in securing Senate approval of the finished product. Measured quantitatively over the years, it has most often simply been neutral, having no results commensurate with the time, trouble, and money required. On the other hand, it exposes members of Congress to the world of multilateral diplomacy and gives them a far better understanding of what U.S. diplomats are up against. From time to time, members of Congress are able to give the U.S. delegation useful advice. Their legislative expertise is of considerable value and the very fact that they have a semi-independent status enables them to inject a certain amount of intellectual ferment into the policy-making process.

There seems no need to try to formalize the arrangements for congressional participation. The number of harmful or neutral cases could be reduced, and the number with beneficial results

could be increased if members of Congress were to limit themselves to conferences of major importance. A rough rule of thumb
might be that congressional participation is desirable only if the
delegation is headed by an officer of Cabinet or sub-cabinet rank.
For conferences of lesser import, but in which Congress still has
an interest, congressional staffs can, and do, serve adequately.

Person-to-Person Relations

The United States prides itself on being a government of laws,
not men. But as laws are made and administered by men, their
nature and relationships with each other are highly important.
The nature of the men is determined by elections, by Presidential
appointments, and by the manner in which the Foreign Service,
the military, and the Civil Service operate to cast up given people
in the upper and upper-middle levels of the bureaucracy. The
relationships existing between these men are the result of a
peculiar mixture of interactions which are partly personal and
partly institutional.

Let us consider first the relationships between members of
Congress, as individuals, and the President as an individual. Up
to and including Franklin Roosevelt, the traditional training
ground for the presidency was the governorship of a large state,
or service in some other executive position, as in the Cabinet.
Since Roosevelt, every President except Eisenhower and every
Vice President except Agnew has served in the Senate. In the six
presidential elections from 1948 through 1968, the two major
parties nominated 17 individuals for the two offices. Eleven of
these (eight out of nine Democrats and three out of eight Republicans) had served in the Senate, and one (Republican vice-
presidential candidate William Miller in 1964) had served in
the House. Five of the eleven (Alben Barkley, John Sparkman,
John Kennedy, Hubert Humphrey, and Henry Cabot Lodge) had
served on the Foreign Relations Committee.

One can postulate a number of reasons for this change from
state houses to the Senate as a source of presidential candidates.

One is that foreign affairs have loomed larger as an area of public concern and that Congress, especially the Senate, provides a better forum for public exposure to foreign affairs than does the governorship of any state. A related factor is that the federal government, through both Republican and Democratic administrations, has assumed an ever-increasing role with respect to matters which used to be left primarily to the states. Whatever the reasons, the notable result is that all but one of the post-World War II Presidents have had that intimate, personal relationship with members of the Senate that comes from membership in the world's most exclusive club. Harry and Jack and Lyndon and Dick, through accident or the magic of the electoral process, have become Mr. President. Familiarity does not necessarily breed contempt, but it does breed a lack of awe. Sometimes, especially in the early years of an administration, it results in a good-humored tolerance. The other side of the coin is that Senators know too much about the human frailties of their recent colleague and are somewhat less impressed than they might otherwise be by his major pronouncements and decisions.

It would seem plausible to expect that a network of close personal friendships in Congress would stand a president in good stead, but the history of the last ten years does not bear this out. Quite apart from whatever differences may exist or develop over policy questions, very shortly after a man becomes president a gulf begins to open between him and almost everybody else. Try as he might to avoid it, he becomes increasingly distracted by the world's most awesome job, he has less and less time for his former pursuits and means of relaxation, and he becomes more and more isolated. Inevitably his new status detracts from whatever personal political leverage he might have had on Capitol Hill. The Senate, which allowed Lyndon Johnson to dominate it as a Senator, finally helped to drive him into retirement as President.

There is a totally different kind of relationship between members of Congress and the upper levels of the career bureaucracy with whom they are most likely to come in contact. As between these two groups of people, indeed, there exists a culture gap almost as wide as the famous credibility gap. As is the case with gaps between other groups (older and younger generations, blacks and whites, hard hats and intellectuals), this one arises in part from different backgrounds and values, but mainly from contrasting life styles; that is to say, from different ways of organizing one's approach to day-to-day problems.

At the level of Assistant Secretary and below, the bureaucracy is enormously specialized, compared to Congress. It is concerned with policy formulation and coordinating executive branch positions, that is, with reaching inter-agency agreements. It tends to suffer from "localitis," either geographically or functionally. It acquires vested interests.

In its dealings with Congress, the bureaucracy is likely to be more concerned with selling a point of view than in exploring a problem. This inevitably leads to a lack of candor, which in turn results in a lack of confidence on the other side. Some upper-middle-level bureaucrats once approached the staff of the Foreign Relations Committee with the question, "What would be the best way to justify the foreign aid program to Congress?" The answer they received was, "Why don't you justify it to Congress the same way you justify it to yourselves?" That this was a rather startling concept to them explains a great deal about what is wrong with executive-legislative relations.

It does not, however, explain *why*. There is perhaps no totally satisfactory explanation. A large part of the trouble no doubt lies in the attitude of a good many bureaucrats who believe in the need for Congress but who are inclined to be critical both of its quality and its performance. The attitude is reciprocated by Congress, which is impatient with bureaucratic procedures and suspicious of bureaucratic motives—an attitude, incidentally, which has been shared by most presidents.

Particularly with respect to budget requests, Congress is convinced that the executive branch normally asks for more than it really needs on the assumption that what it asks for will be cut.

The result is that there is never a real meeting of minds. There is, instead, a stylized fencing match with the executive usually getting a reduced budget.

The bureaucratic attitude stems in part from a curious mixture of fear, contempt, and puzzlement. As a rule Foreign Service officers spend most of their careers outside the United States. Many of them understand the politics of France, Japan, or Brazil a good deal better than they understand the politics of their own country. They deal with their counterparts in foreign bureaucracies, many of whom have their own legislative problems. They frequently see their objectives (for example, land reform in Latin America or larger U.S. appropriations for foreign aid) frustrated by recalcitrant legislative bodies either in the United States or abroad.

Americans who are now in the upper ranks of the Foreign Service were junior officers during the McCarthy era of the early 1950s, and they still bear the marks of that traumatic experience. Some of them tend grossly to mis-estimate political forces in this country and particularly the influence in Congress of the elements with foreign interests, especially the business community. They tend to be influenced by those voices on Capitol Hill which are loudest instead of those which are most powerful or the most sensible.

They should not be faulted too much on this score, because in truth Congress is a house of many voices and is a source of bewilderment to many of its members and closest observers. To paraphrase Shakespeare, the bad that Congress does is apt to make a lasting impression; the good is usually forgotten after the end of each legislative session.

The middle and upper-middle bureaucracy lives in a world which is neatly plotted on organization charts. Congress lives in a world which, by comparison, is wildly disorganized. When members of the two groups talk to each other they rarely share the same universe of discourse and therefore frequently fail to communicate.

Members of the bureaucracy assume a knowledge of detail which Congress does not have. They assume a certain amount of homework which most members of Congress have neither the time nor the inclination to do. They tend to think that more or better staffwork would remedy these deficiencies, just as they tend to think that staffwork saves the day for the Secretary of State and the President. To a degree, they are right, but not so much as they think they are. What they tend to overlook is that members of Congress are intolerably distracted by a thousand things and that they are unwilling—and constitutionally cannot be willing—to delegate many significant responsibilities to their staffs.

To summarize, the bureaucracy tends to take a narrower view than does Congress; it tends to get too involved with facts, to pay more attention to the trees than to the forest. Congress, on the other hand, tends to take a more complicated view; it is at once broader and in certain respects more limited. Congress generally looks at the forest rather than the trees, although individual members may focus more on a few trees even than the bureaucracy—for example, on ethnic groups, or businesses, or certain other economic interests in their constituencies.

Congress also tends to be impatient with the details in which the bureaucracy frequently gets bogged down. And what the bureaucracy does not realize is that one does not have to know everything about a subject to make an intelligent judgment on it. Congress perforce makes judgments, whether intelligent or not. Yet, paradoxically, when Congress tries to learn more—as, for example, about the arrangements under which nuclear weapons are deployed abroad or about some of the activities of the Central Intelligence Agency—the executive branch may well throw up an impenetrable wall of resistance.

Specialists often fall into two traps from which they must be rescued from time to time. In the first place, they tend to lose their perspective. They become so engrossed with their own special areas that they attach more importance to them than they deserve, or they fail to relate them to other important problems that beset us. When I served in the Department of State, for example, the Assistant Secretary in charge of European affairs vigorously defended the interests of his clients in Western Europe, often presenting their views with greater clarity and conviction than the Europeans themselves. In retrospect, reflecting on my own responsibilities for U.N. affairs at that time, I probably attached more significance to the role of the United Nations in American foreign policy than it merited.

In the second place, specialists often become unnecessarily rigid in their thinking. In justifying their own programs they tend to develop certain patterns of thought buttressed by the facts and arguments that prove their points of view. Since they present their cases often, and since their reputations are at stake, they naturally acquire a certain vested interest in the policies they have evolved. Even flabby arguments repeated over and over assume a certain validity. Specialists can thus become prisoners of their own convictions and of established policies; in the circumstances, some may find it very difficult to embrace new ideas.

There are many examples of this attitude of mind in the diplomatic history of postwar Washington. During most of the Eisenhower administration, to take one instance, officials in the Treasury Department were so adamant in their opposition to a multilateral aid program under U.N. auspices, that nothing short of an atomic blast—or a new Secretary of the Treasury—could possibly have shaken their convictions. The Treasury position became so rigid, and its influence in the government so great, that American representatives found it practically impossible even to discuss this subject in U.N. circles.

Clearly, in a democracy specialists need someone to appraise their work in a critical mood, to challenge their basic assumptions, and to make sure their ideas have some genuine relation to the popular will. They need someone with a broad-gauged point of view to raise pointed and even embarrassing questions about their purposes and their objectives. And this is the kind of thing members of Congress are admirably equipped to do.

The White House

New and interesting questions of executive-legislative relations have arisen at the level of the White House staff.

It has traditionally been accepted that the President is entitled to the confidential advice of his intimate friends and personal assistants in addition to the members of his Cabinet. This is the basis of executive privilege, a sort of lawyer-client relationship which has its analogue on Capitol Hill where Congress jealously protects the confidential relationship with its staff employees. Congressional staff members, for example, may not even respond to court subpoenas without formal permission from the branch of Congress by which they are employed.

Historically, the White House staff has been a small and intimate group. One thinks of the very close relationship which existed between Woodrow Wilson and Colonel House, or between Franklin Roosevelt and Harry Hopkins. The seeds of change were planted by the National Security Act of 1947, which created the National Security Council. In accordance with Parkinson's Law, the NSC acquired its own staff, which, over time, has multiplied.

The expansion was delayed somewhat during the Eisenhower years because of the unique relationship with the President that Secretary of State John Foster Dulles had. So much did Dulles have the confidence of the President, and so much was authority delegated to him, that some people accused him of carrying the Department of State and the NSC around in his hat. The charge was facilitated by the fact that his brother Allen served concurrently as Director of Central Intelligence.

The real change began with the advent of President Kennedy and McGeorge Bundy, who were followed in due course by President Johnson and Walt Rostow and by President Nixon and Henry Kissinger. The 1960s saw a steady growth of the National Security Council staff; under Kissinger in 1970, it reached a total of well over 100 people.

During the 1968 election campaign Mr. Nixon had some rather

critical things to say about the Department of State, promising his listeners to revitalize it along the lines of his own thinking. Once in office, he apparently decided instead—in line with his desire to keep the reins in his own hands—to cast the Department in a secondary role, meanwhile substantially expanding the White House staff to deal with foreign-policy questions.

It is in effect a new layer of bureaucracy, interlarded between the President and the departmental bureaucracies of State, Defense, CIA, and the other agencies. Yet it is a bureaucracy peculiarly remote from Congress. By long-standing tradition, the President's National Security Adviser will not accept invitations to appear before congressional committees. He has been perfectly willing to meet individual committee members informally at Washington social functions, at the White House, or even on Capitol Hill when congressional attendance is controlled by the White House and is an across-the-board representation of the leadership rather than the membership of a given committee. More by coincidence than design, the Kissinger staff and some congressional committee staff members know each other and have a variety of haphazard, largely personal contacts.

Critics on Capitol Hill have been quick to point out that this heavy concentration of power in the White House puts the Congress in an anomalous position. With two of the three chief architects of foreign policy protected from congressional inquiry by executive privilege, this could only mean a further erosion of congressional influence and a crippling blow to the system of checks and balances.

The arrangement has thus not been satisfactory to Congress, and what has made it more irksome in recent years is the growing tendency of the National Security Adviser to give background briefings to the press. They are held under ground rules which permit the press to attribute the information disclosed to "high administration officials," but not to name the official who is the source. It is a time-honored practice, the origins of which are lost in the past, but it was certainly done by Bundy and Rostow, as well as by Kissinger. What makes Kissinger's role different is the frequency with which it has been done, particularly at a time when executive-legislative relations have been severely strained. It irritated Senators enormously that representatives of the Associated Press or *The New York Times* can talk to the President's National Security Adviser and the Foreign Relations Committee cannot. It irritated them even more that the transcripts of these backgrounders were available to newspapermen all over Washington, including the representative of *Tass,* but that the State Department long refused to give them to the Senate.

Most Washington observers would probably agree that this practice carries the principle of separation of powers too far. Even Secretary of Defense Laird, when questioned about Kissinger's refusal to make such material available to the Foreign Relations Committee in November 1970, replied that "I would be surprised if information is given to the press that is not being given to Congress." [4] Meanwhile, congressional resentment was not assuaged appreciably by the fact that some members secured copies of the forbidden transcripts from "friendly newsmen." The administration finally took account of these complaints by making the Kissinger transcripts available to the Congress in January 1971.

In addition to understandable pique on this point, Congress sees a shadowy area of executive-branch operations in the role of the NSC staff. Precisely because that role is shadowy, Congress does not understand it and tends to be suspicious. It is no more than a debater's point, without real substance, to say that the NSC staff is a creature of the NSC which in turn is a creature of Congress, and that therefore Congress really ought not to complain about it.

There is a third and subtle element of intra-governmental relations involved here. Aside from the natural imperatives of Parkinson's Law, the NSC staff has proliferated for two reasons. One is that the bureaucracy on which it is supposed to ride herd for the President has itself proliferated in a bewildering array of agencies. It has become an almost impossible task for the Secre-

4. *Washington Post,* November 25, 1970.

tary of State to coordinate the activities of nearly 40 departments and agencies interested in foreign relations. The second, and by far the more important, is that as a group, presidents seem to have a congenital distrust of the bureaucracy in general and of the Department of State in particular. Some Presidents (e.g., Roosevelt and Kennedy) have met this problem by acting as their own Secretaries of State. Some (e.g., Eisenhower) have met it by giving a good deal of authority to a Secretary of State who did not fully trust the Department either. Others (e.g., Johnson and Nixon) have met it by increasing reliance on their White House staffs.

Congress gets involved in the problem partly because its committees in both houses—whether on foreign policy, the armed services, agriculture, and so on—have their favorites in the bureaucracy. The Foreign Relations Committee and the Foreign Affairs Committee, both of which feel shut out from the NSC staff, tend to be protective of the prerogatives of the Department of State. In this view, however, the committees are ambivalent. At times they view the Department with as much distrust as any President does; at times, the distrust becomes despair. But overriding both the distrust and despair is a feeling of exasperation that the Department does not assert its legal prerogatives and authority with greater firmness in dealing with other agencies of the executive branch.

The State Department, for its part, is equally ambivalent in dealing with Congress. Prior to 1965, it used to be said of the Department that it appeased its enemies and ignored its friends on Capitol Hill. Since 1965, the Department can be pardoned for some doubt as to who its friends and enemies in Congress really are.

One thing is clear. Each president has his own style, and Congress does not presume to tell him how to organize his staff. It does seem to many members of Congress interested in foreign policy, however, that a heavy concentration of staff in the White House could lead to a constitutional distortion of considerable proportion. By the same token they believe that if the State Department is to perform its task well, it should be up-graded and strengthened. The remarkable set of proposals which the Department put forward for its own reorganization late in 1970, under the leadership of Secretary Rogers and Deputy Under-Secretary of State William B. Macomber, would appear to be a significant step in that direction.[5]

* * *

When John Foster Dulles became Secretary of State in 1953, he was keenly aware of the congressional difficulties encountered by his predecessor, Dean Acheson. He invited me, as Chief of Staff of the Committee on Foreign Relations, to prepare a list of suggestions to improve the troubled course of executive-legislative relationships. I compiled a comprehensive list, including such ideas as a weekly breakfast meeting between the Secretary of State and the Chairman of the Foreign Relations Committee, *regular* briefings of the two foreign affairs committees, a program of action for the new members of Congress, and regular White House meetings for congressional leaders. "Good gosh," said Mr. Dulles in his best Presbyterian manner, "that's an excellent list but if I do all these things how in the dickens will I find time to run the Department of State?"

Mr. Dulles plaintively reflected the dilemma that has confronted every Secretary of State since World War II. Burdened with monumental responsibilities, they have been called upon to give a good account of themselves in seven directions at the same time: to our friends and allies, our potential enemies, the neutralist countries, the federal bureaucracy, the American people, the President, and the Congress. And in many ways the most important of these is Congress.

The cold statistics only begin to tell the story. Dean Acheson estimates that he devoted approximately one-sixth of his working days in Washington to formal and informal meetings with various congressional committees and groups. Dean Rusk calculates

5. *Diplomacy in the 70's: A Program of Management Reform for the Department of State,* Dept. of State Publication 8551 (Washington, D.C.: G.P.O., 1970).

that he spent at least 50 per cent of his time as Secretary on the domestic aspects of foreign policy—much of it working with Congress. During the first five years of his tenure Rusk appeared in 129 formal committee meetings in the House and Senate. He also met informally with various members of Congress for breakfast and luncheon sessions, briefings and other working meetings on 319 occasions.

Results, unfortunately, cannot be measured by such statistics. Every Secretary of State and every President in the future will find that success in foreign policy will depend to a great extent on finding the right balance of all the factors bearing on their ability to deal successfully with the Congress.

Chapter IV

The Organization of Congress

As the workload of Congress has increased, problems of organization have received growing attention in the press, in popular and scholarly journals, and in Congress itself. Twice within twenty years Congress created a joint committee on organization. The first one fathered the landmark Legislative Reorganization Act of 1946. The second, in 1966, recommended further changes, but unfortunately the bill died in the House Rules Committee. Nevertheless, a group of younger members kept the issue alive, and a new reorganization bill passed the House in 1970 and was also approved by the Senate. Although it made some changes in congressional procedures, it did not fundamentally affect the handling of foreign policy.

Congress is working harder and accomplishing more. But is it accomplishing what it should? Would changes in its organization and its work habits improve the situation? If so, what changes?

Any answer to these questions depends on one's conception of the role of Congress and its relationship to the other branches of government, especially the executive. Herein lies the basis for much of the controversy over congressional organization. Most of the time since 1933, Congress, especially the House, has been more conservative than the President, which has led conservatives to advance proposals aimed at strengthening Congress vis-à-vis the executive. The American Enterprise Institute entitled its studies "Congress: The First Branch of Government,"[1] clearly implying a view of congressional supremacy as distinguished from equality. To hear the many complaints about a rubberstamp Congress, one would think there was something subversive about agreeing with the President.

On the other hand, many liberals have advanced proposals aimed at making it easier to overcome congressional opposition to administration programs. This objective is frequently at bottom and unstated in suggestions as to how Congress could be made more "effective," effectiveness usually being equated with the speed with which Congress acts. These proposals have become somewhat muted in recent years as a result of changing points of view stemming from the controversy over Vietnam. A significant group of members now focuses on how to organize the work so that Congress can deal logically and coherently with the many facets of national security policy, by assembling all relevant information in one place, and thereby truly function as an independent branch of the government.

If the principal objective of congressional reform is to speed up the legislative process and make Congress more efficient, this is precisely what a good many conservatives would vigorously oppose. They prefer to look upon Congress as a restraining influence, a delaying factor, an obstacle to rapid and ill-conceived change. As James J. Kilpatrick puts it, "the 'cumbersome' and 'antiquated' rules of the House and Senate are in fact indispensable adjuncts of a wise and prudent legislative process. They function as brakes upon a powerful machine." And what about reform? "Reform is 100-proof whisky; even the most experienced boozer should sip it with care."[2]

Many proposals from both conservatives and liberals would have the effect of moving the United States closer to a parliamentary form of government. This is implied in the view of

1. The American Enterprise Institute for Public Policy Research, Washington, 1966.
2. "There's a Lot to be Said for the Hill's System," *Washington Evening Star,* Dec. 29, 1970.

Congress as the "first branch of government," as well as in the view of it as the "sapless branch" and especially in the proposals to inject sap into the legislative system.[3] In the first view, carried to its logical conclusion, the Majority Leader of each house would become a sort of prime minister, albeit without much administrative responsibility. In the second view, the majority leadership in general would be strengthened as legislative agents of the President, who himself would be expected to supply leadership for Congress much as a prime minister does for a parliament.

But Congress is not, nor should it be, either the first branch of government or merely an arm of the presidency. It is, under the Constitution, an equal and coordinate branch. As such, its fundamental role is to bring to bear on significant issues an independent judgment independently arrived at through a process which makes it possible for political responsibility to be clearly fixed. This can be done—if Congress really wants to do it—without greatly disturbing its existing organization and procedures. Some very modest steps were taken in the Legislative Reorganization Act of 1970 to strengthen the Legislative Reference Service (renamed the Congressional Research Service) and to provide for recording votes in committees and teller votes in the House.

The problems Congress encounters in foreign policy are, however, largely inherent in the complexity of the world situation and in the constitutional relationship between Congress and the President. The process of meeting these problems could be ameliorated by organizational changes, which will be discussed below, but cannot be solved simply by reorganizing Congress. In short, it is not primarily a question of organization: it is mainly a matter of how Congressmen view their job—of the priorities they assign to the competing claims on their time.

Given the present institutional framework, congressional organization boils down to three principal questions: (1) how the individual member can make better use of his time; (2) how he

3. Joseph S. Clark, *Congress: The Sapless Branch* (New York: Harper & Row, 1964).

can be better informed in the field of foreign policy; and (3) how the inter-related actions of Congress can be better coordinated.

So Little Time

Every Senator is a member of at least two, sometimes more, committees. In addition to the bills handled by these committees, he must have at least a passing acquaintance with the subject matter of other bills debated in the Senate. Furthermore, he has to deal in detail with the problems of his state and his constituents. Members of the House have fewer committee assignments than Senators and fewer constituents, but they have to run for re-election every two years instead of every six.

No member of Congress can possibly do everything he is supposed to do, let alone do it well. For every hour he devotes to problem *A,* he is making a decision, consciously or otherwise, to neglect problems *B, C,* and *D.* The instinct for political survival insures that he will give priority to the problems of his state or district and of his constituents, even though this may not be the best use of his time for the long-run interests of the nation or of his constituents themselves.

After his political chores have been done, a member of Congress can confront the substance of his job. Here he encounters a vast range of problems equalled only in the White House. The Ninetieth Congress enacted 1,002 laws, which dealt with, among other things, space exploration, national parks, foreign assistance, taxes, social security, labor relations, agricultural commodity prices, pollution, health, education, national defense, highway construction, civil rights, and private claims. In addition, the Senate approved the ratification of 41 treaties and confirmed 118,231 presidential nominations ranging from junior Foreign Service officers to members of the Cabinet and the Supreme Court.

The late President John F. Kennedy once commented that "during the 19th century, America had many distinguished senators, presidents, congressmen . . . but most of those men dealt in their entire political life . . . with only four or five major problems. . . . Now the problems swarm across the desks of political leaders of this country."

With this impossible program no member of Congress can be expected—and none pretends—to know very much about all these matters. A few know a good deal about some of them. And some are dealt with routinely without anybody knowing very much, or needing to know very much, about them. The central problem for Congress is to organize its work so that a representative sample of its members knows enough about each of these matters to bring to bear the kind of independent judgment essential to the effective functioning of our checks-and-balances system.

The problem has been approached through dividing congressional work among committees specializing in the broad fields of agriculture, labor, taxes, foreign policy, etc.; but the trouble has been that too many members, especially senators, serve on too many committees and subcommittees. As a consequence, they have had too many conflicting meetings and too many problems they are supposed to master. In the Ninety-first Congress, for example, Senator John Sparkman of Alabama, the second-ranking Democrat on the Foreign Relations Committee, served on four other committees and was chairman of two of them. On the Republican side, Senator Javits served on five other committees and Senator Cooper on four. Of the 15 members of Foreign Relations, only Senators Mansfield and Clifford Case of New Jersey served on just one other committee.

The Reorganization Act of 1946 had dealt with this problem by abolishing a large number of committees and consolidating their functions into fewer committees with broader jurisdiction. It limited each senator to two committees and each representative, with some exceptions, to one. In the ensuing two decades, however, the rules were breached as new committees were created, subcommittees multiplied, and the size of popular committees increased. Senate Foreign Relations, for example, grew from 13 members in 1947 to 19 in 1967, and House Foreign

Affairs from 25 to 36. In 1969, the Senate made a modest start toward reversing the trend. Six committees were reduced in size, notably Foreign Relations from 19 to 15 members and Appropriations from 26 to 24. In the Reorganization Act of 1970, the Senate, where the problem was more acute, again limited its members, with a few exceptions, to two committees.

One obvious step that could be taken to lighten the congressional work load would be to delegate to other bodies or agencies some of the chores which Congress has performed for many years. These include the thankless and time-consuming job of governing the District of Columbia, settling small claims against the government, the appointment of postmasters, handling immigration and naturalization bills, and taking care of applications to West Point, Annapolis, and the Air Force Academy. But here we face yet another striking example of congressional unwillingness to streamline its work program; members complain they have far too much to do yet they refuse to relinquish even those peripheral duties which hang like millstones about their necks.

The Quest for Information

It is much more difficult for members of Congress to inform themselves about questions of foreign policy than about domestic issues. With labor relations, for example, Congress not only has available the Labor Department but also has access to representatives of labor and management who are ready and eager to give helpful information. These voices may be saying different things, but the facts are ascertainable from a variety of sources.

On matters of foreign policy Congress is much more dependent on the executive branch for information. Inevitably this reliance detracts from congressional independence. This is not to say that the executive branch deliberately slants the information it furnishes, though there are occasions when it deliberately withholds information dealing with sensitive subjects. But Congress rarely has available the variety of independent reports which flow to it on domestic issues. It does not have automatically available the means to cross-check reports and assessments, and such cross-checking is indispensable to a sound and independent judgment.

The disparity can never be wholly corrected, because it is ridiculous to suppose that Congress could ever duplicate the worldwide reporting system of the executive branch. Since World War II, however, Congress has paid more attention to developing independent sources of information. The great contribution of the Legislative Reorganization Act of 1946 in this respect was its provision for professional committee staffs chosen on a non-political career basis. Both the Foreign Affairs Committee and the Foreign Relations Committee have followed the letter and the spirit of the provision and have built up small but highly competent staffs.

The establishment of professional staffs has been more responsible than any other factor in developing a proper equilibrium between Congress and the executive branch. In 1945 the staff serving the Foreign Relations Committee—reputedly the most powerful committee on Capitol Hill—was unbelievably small, consisting of a clerk serving on a half-time basis, an assistant clerk, a secretary, and the part-time services of another secretary attached to the chairman's office. In the circumstances the separation-of-powers principle had no real meaning since the committee was almost entirely dependent upon the executive branch for information about foreign policy, for the preparation of committee reports, and for professional assistance of all kinds.

In effect, the creation of the professional staff had a dual impact upon the State Department. It not only brought to the committees of Congress a greater degree of independence, which was sorely needed, but it also made it possible for them to approach their work with a higher degree of professional competence. The result was a net gain for both the Department—which originally had strong misgivings about the desirability of professional staffs—and the Congress. The helpful exchange of ideas and information that ensued at the staff level,[*] and the more efficient operation of the committees generally, laid the ground for a much more fruitful working relationship between the two ends of Pennsylvania Avenue.

It is one of the duties of the staff to bring to the attention of committee members important developments which might otherwise go unnoticed. The staff member himself, of course, is heavily dependent upon the executive branch for information, but he has the time to cultivate other sources as well. He reads the press and the literature more thoroughly than can members of the committee. He may also read the foreign press and reports of foreign radio broadcasts. He talks with private citizens who have personal knowledge of situations in particular countries. He travels abroad himself and reports his observations to the committee.

Members of Congress also travel abroad, either singly or in groups, on the "junkets" about which the press is so cynical. There have been, and doubtless will be, congressional junkets which deserve the criticism they receive; but, by and large, travel serves a very useful purpose. It stimulates interest in foreign affairs and also gives members first-hand information that often proves helpful in dealing with specific problems arising in the House and Senate.

In addition, of course, Congress has available the press and independent experts who testify at hearings or make their own studies under contract with the committees. The Library of Congress and its Congressional Research Service are also available. These great resources, particularly the latter, are not always properly used because many congressmen view them as a means of filling requests from constituents for anything from an Information-Please type question to a student's term paper. The Congressional Research Service needs to be strengthened, but it can never be better than Congress permits it to be.

Ultimately the basic problem is not the collection of facts but their interpretation. Everyone concerned may agree on a given statement of facts about Vietnam, but disagree strongly as to whether these facts justify the conclusion that the United States is winning the war.

The interpretation one puts upon facts is heavily influenced by the way in which they are presented. The Tonkin incident was presented in one way in August 1964; it appeared quite differently three and a half years later after the Foreign Relations Committee staff had meticulously reviewed the original Navy messages. The facts about the Dominican revolution appeared one way to the White House in April 1965; they appeared quite differently to the Foreign Relations Committee after careful scrutiny some months later.

These are the dramatic, unusual examples. Much more common are the day-to-day occurrences which in their totality form the context for the making and execution of foreign policy. Congress does not need to know about these occurrences on a day-to-day basis, but it does need the means of finding out quickly —and independently—when the occasion arises. More staff, in and of itself, is not the answer. It would do little good to produce more staff reports and memoranda—no matter how well prepared —if members do not have time to use them.

The traditional functions of committee staffs are to analyze proposed legislation and (in the case of the Senate) treaties and nominations, to point out new departures or inconsistencies with past committee action, to draft reports on bills and treaties, to help members with amendments and during floor debate. All of these reflect traditional functions of Congress; and regardless of the role it plays in foreign policy, they will continue to be of first importance. But as the congressional role expands, these functions need to be supported by more staff work, especially in the areas of investigation and in-depth reporting.

Investigations serve two broad purposes: They bring to light current situations—for example, the extent of American involvement in Laos as brought out by the Symington subcommittee in 1969–70. Or they shed new light on a past situation—for example, the events in the Gulf of Tonkin or the Dominican Republic. The latter type of investigation presents a peculiar difficulty, not so much in ascertaining the facts as in re-creating the atmosphere of urgency and confusion that existed at the time and making allowance for it in judging the actions taken. Nevertheless, such investigations serve a highly useful purpose in keeping the executive branch honest in the future. The purpose is served, of course, only if the investigation is carried out fairly and objectively, in the spirit of the checks-and-balances system.

Independent reporting in depth by committee staffs may also serve the same purpose. The very fact that such reports are available tends to make the executive branch more forthcoming in its reports to Congress. Indeed, one of the State Department's biggest internal problems is the objectivity of its own reporting —the extent to which reporting may be colored, however subtly, by what the field thinks Washington wants or does not want to hear. The reverse situation also exists—the· extent to which Washington finds what it is looking for in field reports and conveniently ignores what it finds distasteful. It is a common human failing, to which Congress is not immune, but one antidote to it is as much independent cross-checking as is practicable.

To this end a very modest increase in staff would be helpful. It would also be useful for Congress to experiment with modern techniques of data storage and retrieval, which are increasingly being used by the executive branch as well as by private industry.

Much of the information Congress receives about foreign policy is accurate and fair. Some is inaccurate, distorted, misleading or downright false—and as such can have a harmful impact upon the administration's policies and programs unless corrected. Josh Billings once said that "it isn't ignorance that causes all the trouble; it's the fact that people know so darned much that just ain't so." The Bricker Amendment to the Constitution is a notable case in point. It was frequently stated during the debate on that amendment in 1953–54 that the United Nations was, in effect, a huge treaty mill then in the process of concluding more than 200 treaties. A staff check indicated that seven would have been a more accurate number.

Finally, a word of caution should be entered against a tendency to pay too much attention to the execution of policy and too little to the policy itself. For example, an inordinate amount of time is consumed checking reports of waste or corruption in the aid program for Vietnam. The more important question is why there is an aid program in Vietnam at all, and the answer depends less on a detailed knowledge of how each dollar was spent there than on sound judgment and how one views the role of the United States in the world.

The Problem of Coordination

Although the committee system has the advantage of breaking down the totality of matters before Congress into segments of manageable size, it has the consequent disadvantage of dispersing power and fragmenting related subjects. Herein lies one of the chief complaints of the executive branch. "Today, as in the past," the argument runs, "Congress is completely disorganized. It continues to look at foreign policy in an illogical, piece-meal fashion. The one change that is needed on Capitol Hill more than any other is a deliberate effort on the part of congressional leaders to create the kind of machinery that will enable Congress to deal with foreign policy questions in a well-rounded, meaningful way. After all, we are living in the twentieth century."

Admittedly there are good grounds for complaint. Congressional rules are such that neither the Foreign Affairs Committee nor the Foreign Relations Committee has jurisdiction over all the important foreign policy matters. Questions of foreign trade are considered by the House Ways and Means Committee and by the Senate Finance Committee, while exports of agricultural commodities fall within the domain of the Agriculture committees. United States participation in international financial institutions is considered by Foreign Relations in the Senate, but by Banking and Currency in the House. In both houses, many questions of national defense intimately connected with foreign policy are handled by the Armed Services committees. A sizable portion of the field is pre-empted by the Joint Committee on Atomic Energy. And, of course, questions of appropriations are considered separately.

Indeed, as an inevitable consequence of the growing interdependence and complexity of human affairs, there is scarcely a committee in either chamber that does not get involved in foreign policy. Even the committees on the District of Columbia find themselves caught up in international controversy by passing on zoning laws governing the location of foreign embassies in Washington.

This complexity presents an almost impossible problem of coordination—in the executive branch as well as in the legislative. It comes down, in the end, to the question of the priorities and the scale of values of the government and of the society which it serves. In the executive the task of coordination and ordering priorities is performed ultimately in the White House, but every modern President has been troubled by its complexity. In the Congress, the task is theoretically performed in the House and the Senate in leisurely debate, relating one set of interests to another. The process might have worked in the nineteenth century, but it cannot work that way at this point in the twentieth. The great bulk of congressmen are simply too busy, too distracted, too willing to take chances abroad for the sake of scoring points at home. Too many congressmen, in short, are irresponsible in the literal, not the pejorative, sense. If there is a failure of American policy, most likely it will be the President, not Congress, who is held responsible, though some congressional action or omission contributed to the failure. And even if Congress is held responsible, it is even rarer that the responsibility devolves on an individual member—especially if he has been serving the parochial interests of his state or district by his action.

The attempts made by Congress to coordinate its actions and order its priorities have been on the whole feeble and unsuccessful. The Appropriations committees are crude analogies of the Office of Management and Budget of the executive branch, where all spending proposals are supposed to come together, but they have nowhere near its resources or authority. In an effort to improve coordination of fiscal policy the Reorganization Act of 1946 provided for a legislative budget and for a single omnibus appropriations bill. The budget, put together by the appropriate committees of the House and Senate, was to estimate federal receipts and expenditures for the fiscal year and recommend a ceiling on appropriations. These provisions remained in the law until 1970 but were never effective. The only time Congress tried to adopt a legislative budget the attempt bogged down in sharp disagreement between House and Senate. Nor was the experience with an omnibus appropriation bill much better. Such a bill was passed in 1950, but the process was so difficult that those involved vowed never to try it again.

The Legislative Reorganization Act of 1970 provides for the House Appropriations Committee to hold hearings on the budget as a whole. It also provides for the establishment in the executive branch of a standardized information and data processing system for budgetary and fiscal data and for periodic reports to Congress on budget performance. It remains to be seen what effect these modest steps will have.

To secure more effective coordination of congressional action, the Reorganization Act of 1946, as originally drafted, had provided for majority and minority policy committees in both the House and Senate. The provision for these committees in the House was deleted as part of the price exacted by Speaker Sam Rayburn for allowing the House to consider the bill. In the Senate, the committees, serving mainly as arms of the Majority and Minority Leaders, are concerned more with action on the Senate floor than in its committees.

Yet the need for over-all coordination of congressional committees becomes more acute with each passing year. Consideration could well be given to the creation of majority and minority party executive committees in each house. They would be headed by the parties' floor leaders and would be composed of the chairman and the ranking minority member of each committee. Performing the same functions as the policy committees in the Senate, these executive committees would actually do more. They would provide a forum for relating the work of the standing committees and for ordering the priorities among the various interests which these committees reflect. They would decide, or recommend decisions, on the relative weight to be given, for example, to foreign and domestic considerations relating to the export of agricultural commodities. They would perform for Congress functions analogous to those which the National Security Council and the Office of Management and Budget perform for the President. And they could provide a useful mechanism for arbitrating interdepartmental disputes in the executive branch which do not get settled in the White House.

An alternative suggestion, directed to national security policy, would be to create a special Senate committee, composed of the five ranking members of Appropriations, Armed Services, and Foreign Relations, which would pull together the various threads of the budget, the defense program, and foreign policy that are now dispersed among the three committees. The result, it is hoped, would be to give Congress a better over-all view of the cost-effectiveness relationships of various programs and policies in the broad field of defense and foreign affairs.

Yet another possibility might be to provide for congressional membership—with independent staff assistance—on the National Security Council. But the difficult question at once arises as to which members of Congress might be given this important assignment. We shall return to this suggestion in Chapter VII.

Legislative Review

Congress has both a constitutional and statutory duty for the legislative "oversight," or review, of foreign policy. Under the Constitution, foreign-policy powers are shared by the President and the Congress. Under the Legislative Reorganization Act of 1946, each congressional committee is charged to "exercise continuous watchfulness of the execution by the administrative agencies concerned of any laws, the subject matter of which is within the jurisdiction of such committee." The Reorganization

Act of 1970 requires each committee to make a biennial report on its oversight activities (which the Act redesignates as "legislative review").

Primary but by no means exclusive responsibility for overseeing foreign policy is lodged in the two foreign affairs committees. Both have divided themselves into a number of subcommittees, corresponding roughly to the organization of the Department of State. Theoretically, the subcommittees are supposed to keep up with developments in their particular geographic or functional areas. The theory has worked only indifferently in practice, the crucial factor being the interest, of lack of interest, of the subcommittee chairman. Some subcommittees have been quite active; others have been moribund. It is a mistake, however to equate inactivity with indifference. The fact that a committee or a subcommittee does not devote itself to a particular subject does not necessarily mean it is uninterested; it more frequently means that the members are preoccupied with other matters to which they assign a higher priority.

Legislative oversight or review means different things as applied to different agencies and programs. Although the Department of State was created by Congress and there is detailed legislation providing for the Foreign Service, the Department and the Service are really arms of the President and, when he so chooses with respect to policy matters, largely beyond congressional control. The Agency for International Development, on the other hand, is a creature of Congress with no independent existence such as the State Department derives from the President's constitutional power to conduct foreign policy. At annual intervals, AID must go to Congress for renewed life and funds, whereupon Congress performs what one observer has called a tribal rite of loud complaints followed by grudging approval and a reduced budget.

Many members of Congress believe the annual AID review in effect gives Congress more control over foreign aid. (The insistence on this annual review was abandoned in 1969 when Congress passed a two-year aid authorization.) It is true that over the years the reviews have provided occasion for writing a variety of policy directives into the basic legislation. Some of these are helpful guidelines for the administration—e.g., that regional integration or private enterprise or cooperatives should be encouraged. Some are specific limitations, ranging from the reasonable to the ridiculous—e.g., a ceiling on military assistance to Latin America, or a prohibition on aid to Outer Mongolia. But very few of the prohibitions, limitations, and guidelines cannot be circumvented up to a certain point, especially when the President finds it in the national interest to do so. Despite the annual fuss and fury, the Foreign Assistance Act gives the President broad power to use the money appropriated almost any way he desires. On balance, it is hard to see how the program has benefited or suffered very much from the annual congressional scrutiny.

It is much clearer that Congress has suffered. The foreign policy committees in both chambers have been tied in knots for months every year to essentially no useful purpose. Surely this precious time could have been used much more advantageously on other policy problems.

Nor is the annual agony over the aid bill the only time Congress devotes to the subject. Indeed, foreign aid is probably the most investigated activity of the federal government—by the Government Operations and Appropriations committees as well as by Foreign Relations and Foreign Affairs, by the General Accounting Office, and by the State Department's Inspector General for Foreign Assistance. Some of the investigations have led to legislation or to important policy changes. But many of them have done no more than to document what could reasonably have been presumed without an investigation—namely, that in a program of this size, operating in countries with inadequate administrative structures, there is going to be a certain amount of waste. It is perhaps useful; but because of the time required for investigations, much of the documentation comes long after the fact, sometimes even after the administration has corrected the conditions which gave rise to the waste.

Perhaps the most difficult area of legislative oversight is that of national defense, the military establishment, and the intelligence community. The affairs of the Department of Defense fall within the legislative jurisdiction of the Armed Services committees but are intimately related to foreign policy. And like foreign policy, defense is an area of shared presidential-congressional powers. Congress can declare war and is to provide for the armed forces, but the President is their Commander-in-Chief.

It is obvious that executive powers in this field have been expanding steadily while congressional powers have been contracting. Twice since World War II, the President has involved the United States in what is war in every sense but the legal one requiring a declaration of war from Congress.

With respect to less dramatic questions of defense policy, Congress has been much more assertive though with scarcely more results. During the Kennedy and Johnson administrations, it repeatedly clashed with Secretary of Defense McNamara whose rigorous application of the principles of cost-effectiveness bruised congressional feelings. Through overriding or attempting to override McNamara's decisions, Congress made it more difficult for him to exercise civilian control of the armed forces; but Congress did not do much to exercise such control itself. One reason for its behavior is the traditional bias of the Armed Services committees in favor of the uniformed services—a bias assiduously cultivated by the services. It is a sad commentary on congressional parochialism that a proposal to close a navy base in Brooklyn excited far more interest than building one in Cam Ranh Bay.

The Intelligence Community

With respect to legislative supervision of the intelligence community, the situation appears to be even less satisfactory. That "community" consists principally of the Central Intelligence Agency, the Defense Intelligence Agency, the National Security Agency, the Bureau of Intelligence and Research of the Department of State, and on some matters, the Federal Bureau of

Investigation and the Atomic Energy Commission. In Congress, CIA, DIA, and NSA are under the jurisdiction of the Armed Services committees; State's Bureau of Intelligence and Research (INR) is under the Foreign Relations and Foreign Affairs committees; and the FBI is under the Judiciary committees. The Appropriations committees, of course, have an interest that goes across the board, as do the committees on Government Operations. None of these committees has fully met its responsibilities of legislative oversight; perhaps, given the wide dispersal of jurisdiction, none of them can.

In each house the Appropriations and Armed Services committees have subcommittees on the CIA. In the Senate, mainly because of overlapping membership, these subcommittees have customarily met jointly in recent years. So far as is known, the Armed Services committees have given little or no attention to DIA and NSA; nor have the Judiciary committees given any to the FBI, whose Director is generally held on Capitol Hill to stand only a little lower than the angels. Nor has Foreign Relations or Foreign Affairs taken any great interest in State's INR.

The main problem, obviously, is the CIA, which engages in more of the kind of foreign operations that are likely to backfire. No one can doubt that these operations—the U-2 flights and the Bay of Pigs fiasco are prime examples—play a significant and sometimes highly disruptive role in foreign policy. There have been repeated suggestions that Congress establish a joint committee on the CIA similar to the Joint Committee on Atomic Energy. One such proposal, sponsored principally by Senator Mansfield, came to a vote in the Senate in 1956 and was defeated 27–59. In 1966, under the principal sponsorship of Senator Eugene McCarthy, the Foreign Relations Committee approved a resolution to create a select Senate Committee on Intelligence Operations, to be composed of three members each from Appropriations, Armed Services, and Foreign Relations. The effect would be to broaden the membership of the existing subcommittee on CIA by adding three members from the Foreign Relations Committee, and to broaden its jurisdiction by taking in the rest of the intelligence community. This proposal was also shunted aside by a vote of 61–28 to refer it to the Armed Services Committee where it quietly died. At least a part of the intended result was attained, however, in January 1967 when three members of the Foreign Relations Committee were invited to sit with the Armed Service-Appropriations subcommittee. This change has not made any noticeable practical difference because the subcommittee has rarely met.

A major problem in overseeing intelligence operations is security. Although Congress is frequently charged with leaking like a sieve, the congressional record on security, at least in these highly classified areas, compares favorably with that of the executive branch. The Joint Committee on Atomic Energy has access by law to the vast array of secrets of the Atomic Energy Commission, and this has not created any insurmountable security problems. Nor, for that matter, have such problems arisen from the subcommittees assigned to watch over CIA.

What is basically involved is something it pains the Senate to talk about—personality differences and bureaucratic jealousies. To be blunt about it, and perhaps to overstate it, neither the CIA nor the people who now watch over it fully trust the people who want to watch over it; and the people who want to watch over it do not fully trust either the agency or its present watchers. Although the executive branch strongly opposed earlier proposals to establish a joint committee, it has more recently agreed that arrangements for legislative oversight are a matter of the internal organization of Congress. For its part, CIA has made plain that it prefers the existing arrangements.

There is a suspicion in some quarters that the existing subcommittees do not subject CIA to the rigorous questioning which might be expected from the two foreign affairs committees. A good many skeptics in Washington doubt that the CIA is adequately supervised even within the executive branch, in addition to the many more who question the adequacy of congressional supervision. Although an outsider cannot be certain, there is some evidence to support these conclusions, at least as far as

Congress is concerned. The most significant weakness, perhaps, is the lack of staff for the subcommittees which are now supposed to oversee CIA. The two subcommittees in the Senate have only one part-time staff member, who is already heavily burdened with his duties as chief of the professional staff of the Armed Services Committee. It is quite unrealistic to think that a few busy legislators can learn enough about the agency to ask the right questions without thorough staff work. Furthermore, because of the CIA's intimate involvement in foreign policy, both the staff and the members ought to approach its activities with foreign-policy considerations very much in mind.

Another bit of evidence is that when something goes wrong as a result of CIA activity, Congress does not look to the Armed Services-Appropriations subcommittees for explanations; it looks to the Foreign Relations Committee. It was Foreign Relations that held hearings on the U-2 incident in 1960 and the Bay of Pigs episode in 1961. Moreover, Foreign Relations did not go to the Armed Services Committee for an explanation of CIA's role in these enterprises; it went directly to CIA itself. This is in sharp contrast to the way Congress approaches atomic energy matters, on which it always seeks guidance first from the Joint Committee on Atomic Energy.

It may be admitted that present congressional arrangements for oversight of the intelligence community are inadequate without concluding that any of the proposed changes would necessarily avoid the mistakes of the past. There is certainly no guarantee that congressional watchdogs would be any wiser or would exercise any more vigilance or foresight than National Security Council watchdogs. Some of CIA's mistakes, however, have stemmed from the agency's own overconfidence that it could carry off a particular project or activity. It is reasonable to suppose that more searching questioning of plans at earlier stages would provide a much-needed antidote. Greater congressional oversight might accomplish this purpose and might also serve to protect CIA from some of the undeserved criticism it now receives.

In summary, many of the shortcomings in legislative review exist because Congress wants it that way. Congress as a whole would rather not have the responsibility of checking on some of the more dubious activities of the CIA. By the same token, many Senators would rather not have the responsibility of committing themselves to a treaty in the negotiating stages. They would rather abdicate the duty of advice in order to retain more freedom to withhold consent at a later stage.

The Seniority System

For years, the seniority system has been highly criticized by most students of Congress, while it was taken as holy writ by congressmen themselves. Then suddenly in 1970, largely as a result of bipartisan agitation by younger members of the House, it became respectable, indeed almost fashionable, to question seniority. Both party organizations in the House appointed committees to study the problem. Critics of the seniority system usually concentrate on pointing out its defects; defenders usually content themselves with arguing the defects of alternative proposals.

The system has two principal disadvantages: it puts older, sometimes senile, men in positions of power, and it may make committee chairmen of men who are completely out of tune with their party. As Tom Wicker of *The New York Times* pointed out in the spring of 1970: "seniority brings gavels indiscriminately to anyone who can hang on long enough." [4]

Since World War II, the average age of the chairmen of the Foreign Affairs Committee when they left office has been 69; the comparable figure for chairmen of the Foreign Relations Committee is 75. On the House committee, Representative Eaton of New Jersey served when he was 80; Representatives Sol Bloom of New York and John Kee of West Virginia were each 76 when they relinquished the chairmanship. On the Senate side, Senator Connally stepped down at 75 and Senator George at 78. The

4. *The New York Times*, March 17, 1970.

record is held by Senator Theodore Green, who resigned as chairman when he was 91 and then continued as a member of the committee for two more years. In comparison with their predecessors, the present incumbents—Senator Fulbright and Representative Morgan—were relatively young men when they assumed the chairmanships of their respective committees in 1959.

The chairmanship of any major committee is a tough and taxing job, and this is especially true of Foreign Relations and Foreign Affairs. Even though a given individual is in good health, age inevitably takes a toll in physical vigor, acuteness of vision and hearing, memory, and mental alertness. It is therefore sometimes suggested that Congress fix an arbitrary age—70, for example—beyond which a committee member could not serve as chairman, though he could remain a member for as long as he could get elected. This rule would, of course, be discriminatory, both against the member and against his state or district. The only way to avoid such discrimination would be by amending the Constitution so as to set maximum as well as minimum ages for members of Congress—an action that is highly unlikely.

Because of the way it works, the seniority system accentuates the problem of age in committee chairmen; but the problem is broader than that, especially in the Senate. In the Ninety-first Congress, for example, 9 of 15 members of the Foreign Relations Committee (including all of the Republicans) were older than the chairman. While age should bring a certain amount of wisdom, in a nation where half the people are 27 years of age or under it does seem a little incongruous that our foreign-policy machinery should be so heavily dominated by senior citizens.

On the other hand, it is true that many members, because of their long tenure, bring a continuity of experience and an expertise to their posts which cannot normally be matched in the top echelons of the Department of State or the Department of Defense. The late Senator Richard Russell of Georgia, for example, served as chairman or ranking Democratic member of the Senate Armed Services Committee from 1951 until 1969. Representatives Walter Judd of Minnesota and Frances Bolton of Ohio served as members of the House Foreign Affairs Committee for some two decades, and among the members in 1971 were a number (including Wayne Hays of Ohio, Thomas Morgan of Pennsylvania and Clement Zablocki of Wisconsin) who had served from 15 to 25 years. The interest of Senator J. William Fulbright of Arkansas in foreign policy goes back to 1943 when, as a member of the House, he introduced his resolution calling for the participation of the United States in a postwar international organization. His service thus overlaps the tenure of Secretaries of State Rogers, Rusk, Herter, Dulles, Acheson, Marshall, Byrnes, Stettinius, and Hull. Senator Bourke Hickenlooper of Iowa, before his retirement in 1968, participated actively in the work of the Senate Foreign Relations Committee and the Joint Committee on Atomic Energy for many years. Such members, equipped with a wide knowledge of past policies and programs, can and do make valuable contributions to the foreign-policy process. The story of Representative Carl Vinson of Georgia, who served as Chairman of the House Armed Services Committee for many years, is illuminating. When asked about the report that he might resign his seat to become Secretary of Defense, Mr. Vinson replied: "I would rather run the Pentagon from here."

Perhaps more important than age is the fact that a chairman selected according to seniority may be seriously out of step with his party and with majority opinion in Congress or the country as a whole. A most conspicuous recent example was the attitude of Senator James O. Eastland of Mississippi, chairman of the Judiciary Committee, toward President Johnson's civil rights program. In this case, the administration found ways to overcome Eastland's opposition, but a committee chairman can be highly obstructive if he wants to be.

Another contemporary example is Senator Fulbright, an articulate dissenter from much of the foreign policy of both the Johnson and Nixon administrations. Despite his vigorous opposition to the Vietnam war and the Dominican intervention, Fulbright has not, however, used his position to thwart proper consideration of the administration's foreign-policy measures by the committee or by the Senate.

It should be noted that before a member of Congress can begin to accumulate seniority on a committee and rise toward the chairmanship, he first has to become a member of the committee. The method of making committee appointments is, therefore, of considerable importance. Until the middle 1950s, this was done by both parties strictly on a basis of seniority. One of the great changes wrought by Lyndon Johnson as Majority Leader was to breach this system, so far as the Democrats were concerned; and Senate Republicans have since modified the seniority rule to a lesser degree. The current practice in the Senate, which differs between the parties only in detail, is that each senator will be assigned to one major committee. This is a vast improvement over the old practice whereby junior senators were relegated to the committees on the District of Columbia and the Post Office until they acquired enough seniority to demand a position on Finance or Foreign Relations.

The door was opened a tiny crack in January 1971, shortly after the new Congress convened. House Democrats and Republicans both agreed to modify the seniority system so that, in effect, the selection of committee chairmen would henceforth be subject to the approval of the party caucus. Liberal Democrats failed, however, to impose a 70-year age limit for committee chairmen and to restrict their service to four two-year terms.

While the action taken in the House is far from revolutionary, it is a step forward. How much practical difference it will make remains to be seen. In this connection it is of more than passing interest to note that the chairmen approved in January 1971 were precisely those individuals who would have been eligible on a strict seniority basis. Nevertheless, the new arrangements do provide a means, not previously available, for by-passing seniority in extreme cases. Meanwhile, on the other side of Capitol Hill, the Senate Democratic caucus gave proponents of change further encouragement by appointing a committee to study the seniority question.

The other side of the argument also deserves to be made. In emphasizing that the seniority principle will often cast up as committee chairman someone totally out of sympathy with the President's program or with a party line, critics are really criticizing the lack of party discipline which is so characteristic of American politics. The seniority system clearly makes it more difficult to enforce party discipline because it tends to protect from reprisal party intransigents who have seniority. Implicit in criticism of the system is the assumption that parties ought to be united—that the President's party ought to control Congress, or at least stick together if it does not control it, and that the opposition party ought to be monolithic in its opposition.

This comes close to a description of the parliamentary system, and it ignores the American principle of separation of powers and also the fact that the opposition party may have a majority in one or both houses. It would be more in keeping with the spirit of our Constitution to argue that both parties and the individual members in Congress ought to hold themselves independent of the executive and decide issues *ad hoc* rather than on the basis of the President's point of view. Because of the special role of the Senate with respect to treaty-making and of Congress as a whole with respect to declarations of war, this perhaps applies *a fortiori* so far as foreign policy is concerned. Some would go so far as to say that the chairman of the two foreign policy committees ought to play the role of devil's advocate vis-à-vis the President and the Secretary of State. This is overstating the case. But neither should he be the Senate spokesman for the administration, as he was considered to be during the 1930s and 1940s. To give him his position—and to protect him in it—by virtue of seniority is not necessarily to insure that he is either one or the other; that depends almost totally on the man. But the seniority system certainly gives him a measure of independence which he would not otherwise have.

The *Federalist Papers* are full of warnings against "factions" —i.e., political parties. It is hard to see how we could do without them, but it should also be recognized that strict party discipline is incompatible with the separation of powers. It is a part of the American political genius that an in-between system has been made to work reasonably well, despite its creaks and rattles. On balance, it would seem that what is called for is substantial modification, rather than complete abandonment, of the seniority system.

Interparliamentary Meetings

In recent years, Congress has become increasingly involved in international interparliamentary groupings of one kind or another which have not yet received the attention they deserve. There are at least eight groups which meet more or less regularly: the worldwide Interparliamentary Union; two regional associations in the Western Hemisphere and one in the North Atlantic area; bilateral arrangements with Canada, Mexico, and the United Kingdom; and the Commonwealth Parliamentary Association, composed of parliaments of the British Commonwealth, to whose meetings Congress is regularly invited though it is not a member. In addition, there are a good many special groups, some of them on a one-time-only basis, and members of Congress also occasionally attend meetings of the Consultative Assembly of the Council of Europe.

The argument in favor of such meetings is that they contribute to better mutual understanding. To a degree they do. Nobody really makes an argument in principle against them any more. Purists tend to look askance at them, for they always carry a degree of danger that legislators, as a result of such gatherings, may tend to by-pass their own foreign offices. Experience has shown this danger to be considerably less than was once feared. On the contrary, experience—particularly with the U.S.-Mexico and the U.S.-Canada groups—has shown that these meetings often strengthen the hands of foreign offices in dealing with their own legislatures. There seems little doubt, for example, that the Chamizal Treaty with Mexico had smoother sailing in the Senate because a number of key Senators had been exposed to the Mexican position in prior interparliamentary discussions.

The more compelling argument against such meetings—and particularly against their proliferation—is that Congress is not equipped, and is probably unable to equip itself, to participate in them adequately. This is not a question of staff, though the Congress could usefully employ more staff to work on such matters. It is not a question of organization, though this could probably be improved. The root of the matter is that members of the U.S. Congress have a great deal more to do than the members of almost any other parliamentary body in the world. With very rare exceptions, it is next to impossible to find enough able members of Congress who are willing to take the time to attend an interparliamentary conference, to participate in it actively, and to do a modicum of homework beforehand. The problem becomes more acute as sessions of Congress become longer.

There seems to be no graceful way in which Congress can reduce the number of interparliamentary commitments which it has already made. It should certainly not add any new ones, and it should take the existing ones more seriously.

Congressional organization for participation in interparliamentary meetings should be centralized to a greater degree. Permanent, full-time staff is needed, particularly for administrative arrangements, as these have become a burden on the staffs of the Senate Foreign Relations and the House Foreign Affairs committees.

* * *

In Washington it is often said that we don't solve problems, we just manage them. This maxim has a certain relevance to the difficulties and complexities of the role of Congress in foreign policy. These do not stem primarily from the organization of that august body. They could, however, be alleviated by certain badly needed reforms in congressional organization and procedures.

No one can doubt that Congress needs a good face-lifting job. For years it has been creaking along, bogged down by antiquated customs and procedures and seriously handicapped by its own unwillingness to enact needed reform. If its members demand a greater role in foreign affairs they should be willing to pay the price—a modernization of Congress so it can more effectively carry its share of the foreign policy burden. As a minimum they should be willing to: (1) organize their work program so that certain members have more time for foreign policy; (2) strengthen the capacity of Congress for legislative review; (3) deal more seriously than they have with the problem of seniority; (4) develop more independent sources of information on foreign affairs; (5) take effective steps to protect the integrity of classified information; and (6) provide for more effective coordination of foreign policy matters within Congress.

Measures like these certainly would make it easier for Congress to form its own judgment, relatively independent of the executive. But they would not assure such a judgment by any means. In the last analysis, that is dependent on the caliber of the individuals the American people elect to Congress and on the conception these individuals have of their role in the American government.

Chapter V

Congress and Public Opinion

In evaluating the congressional role in foreign policy, the one thing never to be forgotten is that Congress is a political body. Every member wins his seat through political action. If he remains there, as most hope to, it will be through political action.

This very natural desire to remain in office is frequently criticized. The phrases "he's looking for votes" or "he's playing politics" are usually said scornfully. Yet any informed person's list of the greatest statesmen the United States has produced would also include the best politicians. In the Congress, nobody has a chance to prove himself as a statesman until he has first proved himself as a politician—until he has been elected, and more important, re-elected to office. The practice of politics is not to be denigrated. It is essential to the democratic process and to self-government.

Foreign Policy and Elections

A member of Congress has to be concerned constantly over the next election (though a Senator may be forgiven a few lapses during the first year or two of his term). If a member is not so concerned, it will be said, depending on one's point of view, that he "has great political courage" or that he is "contemptuous of public opinion." In either case, it will almost certainly be said of him after not very long that he is a former member of Congress.

Congressional elections are determined by the state of public opinion on a given day every two years. So far as an individual member of Congress is concerned, the determinants of elections are further limited to the state of public opinion in a given geographic area. Congress is not only a political body; it is a parochial body as well, since each member must serve parochial interests.

Senator Tom Connally's reaction to a visit paid him by the Ambassador from Greece in 1947 is, if not typical, at least illustrative. The Senator was closeted with some important constituents from Texas. When told the Ambassador had stopped by to thank him for his leadership in securing congressional approval of the program of aid to Greece and Turkey, the Senator replied half seriously and half in jest, "Hell, there aren't any votes for me in Greece. Tell the Ambassador I'm very sorry but I won't be able to see him today."

"Public opinion" may be quite different for individual members of Congress. Although regional and cultural diversity within the United States is diminishing as we become a more mobile and integrated nation, these differences still exist. Iowa farmers see the world in one way, and Detroit automobile workers in quite another. The primary concerns of the Boston Irish differ from those of the Poles in Chicago or the Chinese in San Francisco. There are basic economic differences as well. Wheat and cotton farmers, who rely heavily on exports, have a different view of foreign trade policy than do fruit and vegetable growers who feel threatened by imports. Similar variations in viewpoint exist between the export-oriented machinery industry and the protectionist textile industry. International oil companies may want to import more petroleum—as do residents of New England who wish to buy it at lower than current prices—while the oil producers of Texas and the coal producers of West Virginia understandably want to import less.

These are essentially parochial interests, of immediate importance only to limited groups. Any one of them taken by itself is likely to have worldwide, or even nationwide, repercussions though the sum of several or all of them may determine an important national policy. Congress, being itself a parochial body, reflects these interests.

Because Congress does devote much attention to parochial interests, those who do not share them frequently assign them more importance than they actually have in determining the broad sweep of foreign policy. Most foreign policy issues before the Congress are at two quite different levels. At one level—that which receives the widest attention—are the transcendent issues of war or peace: American involvement in Vietnam, U. S. relations with the Soviet Union, the Middle East conflict, and generally the ideological issues with a high emotional content. At the other level, accounting for the larger number by far, are the less dramatic issues which, in their totality, nonetheless have an important influence on the shape of our policy and world posture. These are issues such as foreign aid, or international monetary arrangements, about which public opinion is somewhat apathetic or to which it assigns a low priority in the scale of values against which it ranks candidates for Congress. Moreover, these issues are almost always more controversial in Congress than in the country at large, a fact which leads many members to exaggerate the intensity of public opinion about them.

The conventional wisdom on Capitol Hill is that foreign aid is generally unpopular, but a persuasive argument can be made that votes for foreign aid have been a crucial factor in the defeat of few, if any, members. The cases most often cited are those of Senators Connally of Texas and George of Georgia, each of whom retired from the Senate while serving as chairman of the Foreign Relations Committee rather than risk defeat. But in each case, the Senator's pro-foreign-aid record was only one—and probably not the most important—of a congeries of factors such as age, long absence from his state, and general identification with international affairs rather than with the home front.

It has been said that politicians make decisions based on what is good for the next election; statesmen make them based on what is good for the next generation. As far as Congress is concerned this maxim would seem to apply more to domestic issues than to foreign policy.

The moral to be drawn is that with respect to most foreign-policy issues, always excepting the transcendent ones dealing directly with peace or war, a member of Congress who has assiduously watched after the parochial interests of his state or district can do largely as he pleases. He can even afford the luxury of being a statesman from time to time. But although he can vote for a foreign aid bill with impunity, he probably has more to gain in purely political terms from opposing it. This is especially true with respect to those issues on which public opinion is, for all practical purposes, nonexistent. The International Coffee Agreement is a good example. There is impressive evidence that it has had little if any impact on the price of coffee in the supermarkets, and most American coffee-drinkers are blissfully unaware of its existence. Almost any Senator, therefore, can vote for the agreement with complete impunity because his constituents will pay no attention; but a Senator who chooses to oppose it can get some headlines—a political plus—without setting up an adverse reaction at home.

At any given time and place, the state of public opinion is determined by a very complex set of factors and manifests itself in equally complicated ways. So intricate are these relationships that it is frequently difficult to separate cause and effect, or to identify any single factor as the crucial determinant. Rarely are politicians confronted with an issue so vital and so clear that they are required to choose between sacrificing their careers or their principles. That this does not happen more often is a part of the genius of the American political system. One reason lies in the diversity of American society. Another reason lies in the fact that Congress does not only follow public opinion; it also creates and leads it.

Congress as a Forum for Public Debate

"Even more important than legislation," wrote Woodrow Wilson, "is the instruction and guidance in political affairs which the people might receive from a body which kept all national concerns suffused in a broad daylight of discussion." [1]

The Senate is far better equipped than the House is for the role Wilson had in mind because of its smaller size, its tradition of unlimited debate, and the disrespect which it habitually pays to its pallid rule of germaneness. So far as foreign policy is concerned, the Constitution also assigns a more important role to the Senate, where historically the great debates on foreign policy have taken place.

Most observers would probably agree that the general level of Senate debate has deteriorated in recent years. For one thing, most Senators are less interested in debate than they used to be. The number of pages they fill in the *Congressional Record* has steadily grown, disproportionate even to the increasing length of their sessions. But most pages are filled with prepared speeches, or reprints of newspaper or magazine articles, or of somebody else's speeches, wildly irrelevant to whatever happens to be the pending business. Complex issues from outer space to inner cities come before the Senate in such bewildering array that even a modern Benjamin Franklin could not have very much that was sensible to say on many of them.

The trouble goes deeper than this. Senators are far busier than they used to be. On any given afternoon when the Senate is in session there are likely to be half a dozen activities which Senators would find both more agreeable and more profitable than sitting in the Senate Chamber. In order to accommodate them, the leadership, especially since the days when Lyndon Johnson was Majority Leader, has tried to schedule most of the important business on the basis of unanimous consent agreements either fixing a time for voting or limiting debate so that a Senator will know with reasonable certainty when a vote will be taken. He can then come to the Chamber for the vote and go about his other affairs with a minimum of inconvenience. The unanimous consent agreement has proven to be a most effective device for expe-

1. Woodrow Wilson, *Congressional Government* (Boston: Houghton Mifflin Co., 1913), p. 297.

diting Senate action on legislation, but it has been a stultifying influence on debate—not so much through time limitations as through the incentive it gives Senators to be absent from the Chamber.

Great speeches are still made in the Senate, but they are usually read to a nearly empty Chamber and their impact, including their impact on other Senators, comes from the attention they receive in the press and on television. A quarter of a century ago it was not unusual for 60 or 70 Senators to be present to hear Senator Arthur Vandenberg discuss an important foreign policy issue; yet no more than three or four heard Senator Fulbright's delivery of his really remarkable address on "Old Myths and New Realities." Changing times rather than the quality of speeches accounts for the disparity in the audiences they attract.

To say that the Senate is no longer the scene of great debates, however, is not to say that it no longer provides an important forum for public discussion. It still is the forum, the difference being that the debates take place nowadays not so much in the Senate itself as in its committees and the mass media. During the period 1966–68, when the country was becoming ever more sharply divided over Vietnam, the issue was much discussed in the Senate. Several important Senators made thoughtful speeches on both sides of the question, but these seldom were more than a mere reading of prepared statements. Sometimes other Senators, who were on the same side of the issue and had been forewarned, would be on hand to lend moral support. But rarely was there any spontaneity in give-and-take discussion. That came in hear-ings before the Foreign Relations Committee.

As much as a classic great debate in the Senate, these hearings performed the essential function which Woodrow Wilson outlined, of keeping "national concerns suffused in a broad daylight of dis-cussion." And in some respects the hearings performed this func-tion even better than a Senate debate. They brought to the discussion not only Senators, but the principal protagonists of the administration's policy. The verbal exchanges between Sen-ator Fulbright and Secretary Rusk were more impressive than any level of debate which could possibly have been attained in the Senate itself, simply because one of the parties was the Secretary of State. The hearings also made it possible to bring into the discussion recognized experts of stature from outside the government, for example, former Ambassadors George Kennan and Edwin O. Reischauer. The extensive television coverage of the hearings made more people aware of the ramifications of the issue than would have been the case if the same debate had taken place in the Senate itself where television is not allowed and where non-members cannot participate.

Like a great debate in the Senate, the hearings ranged beyond the immediate issue at hand to probe deeply into the role of the United States in the world, the nature of revolution, and the relative powers of the executive and legislative branches. Beginning at a time when few in authority were publicly questioning the premises of the administration's policy, they lent respectability to dissent and provided something of an outlet—albeit largely vicarious—for the frustrations of the dissenters on college campuses and elsewhere around the nation. It has been reported that Senator Eugene McCarthy made his decision to run for the presidency after listening to Undersecretary of State Katzenbach's defense of the war-making powers of the executive in a hearing of the Foreign Relations Committee. In any event, it seems not too much to say that the committee's hearings on Vietnam and related issues during the period 1966–68 contributed significantly to President Johnson's decision not to seek re-election and to the changes in American policy which led to the Paris peace negotiations.

By the same token and for the same reasons, the hearings which the Foreign Relations Committee's Subcommittee on Disarmament held on the ABM in 1969 shed a great deal more light on that subject than did the ensuing debate in the Senate, in no small part because of the technical expertise of many of the witnesses.

For congressional hearings to have this effect, however, they must be carried on in public. There are occasions when the national interest dictates that hearings be held in private session.

The considerations involved are of two kinds. There are the cases in which the subject matter does not involve classified information even though it may be highly sensitive in nature. This is what led the administration stoutly to resist a public airing of its Vietnam policy. One of the premises of its policy was that a firm, unyielding stand, backed by a united country, would eventually lead Hanoi to capitulate, or at least to negotiate. To the degree that the policy was questioned—especially by responsible leaders in American life—the premise would be undermined. One does not have to follow the argument very far, however, before one denies the right of open debate in a free society. The Foreign Relations Committee hearings in themselves did not create division in the United States although they certainly contributed to it; they recognized the fact of its existence and gave dissent a respectable outlet. The Nixon administration, with somewhat more success than Johnson, has continued to emphasize the importance of a show of national unity which does not exist.

On another level arise the problems of dealing with classified information in connection with *ex post facto* congressional examination of foreign policy decisions. For example, in 1957 following the Suez crisis, President Eisenhower asked Congress for the so-called Middle East resolution giving him broad authority to act in that part of the world. In the Senate, the resolution was referred to the Foreign Relations and Armed Services committees sitting jointly, and in the course of their consideration, they asked the Department of State for a fully documented account of the development of United States policy on the Middle East since 1946. Before the committees called a halt several months later, the Department had delivered something more than twenty bulky volumes of documents, ranging from public treaties to the most sensitive telegrams and White House memoranda. This mass of material was examined in full by the staff of the Committee and in major part by Senators Fulbright and Knowland, who came to opposite conclusions about the wisdom of U.S. policy respecting the Aswan Dam. Both agreed only that reasonable men could come to different conclusions on the basis of the secret evidence. Fulbright commented particularly on the inhibitions of secrecy:

> The conclusions which I have reached cannot be subject to the jury of public opinion as long as the documents supporting those conclusions must remain classified. It is impossible for the press, for members of the public, and for students of foreign policy in the Middle East to determine whether my conclusions are sound and whether our actions which I believe contributed directly to the seizure and closure of the Suez Canal were reasonable or unreasonable in the light of the facts available to the Department of State. . . . It is an unsatisfactory state of affairs when the American people have no basis upon which to judge whether the Secretary of State acted responsibly or irresponsibly in withdra ing the offer of the United States to help finance the Aswan Dam.[2]

This was an extreme case. More frequently, the bulk of the material furnished to a congressional committee can be declassified and published. When the Senate Foreign Relations and Armed Services committees held joint hearings on the military situation in the Far East following President Truman's 1951 action in relieving General MacArthur of his command, arrangements were made for the transcript to be censored on the spot by high-ranking military officers and released to the press within an hour or so. A similar arrangement was followed at the time of the Foreign Relations Committee's inquiry into the U-2 incident in 1960. In both cases, the public airing of most of the facts contributed to taking much of the heat out of an extremely explosive issue.

On the other hand, nothing has ever been published of the committee's inquiries into the Bay of Pigs incident in 1961 or the Dominican Republic intervention in 1965 although the essential parts of both stories have become public from other sources. The Symington subcommittee's hearings on Laos in 1969–70 were published in censored form, but only after prolonged and

2. 103 *Congressional Record* 14701–14710, esp. 14708 (Aug. 14, 1957).

frequently acrimonious argument between the subcommittee and the executive branch.

Most members of Congress think, with some reason, that the executive branch tends to over-classify information and that its decisions on declassification are sometimes based on considerations other than national security. On this score, public opinion probably sides with Congress; certainly the press does. On the other hand, most officials of the executive branch think, again with some reason, that members of Congress are unnecessarily careless with classified information.

The magnitude of the problem, however, is frequently exaggerated. There are many fundamental questions of foreign policy (e.g., the basic national interest of the United States in Southeast Asia) which can be quite adequately debated without access to secret intelligence. The questions which depend on such access (e.g., the Cuban missile crisis) are usually of such a nature that they must of necessity be decided initially at least by the executive, and the congressional role, if any, comes after the fact. It is true that selected members of Congress may be consulted during the decision-making process, or at least informed prior to public announcement of the results of the process. But this is not at all the same thing as a public airing of the issue either through a great debate in Congress or through committee hearings designed to serve the same purpose.

With respect to decisions like those on the Bay of Pigs, the Cuban missile crisis, or the Dominican intervention, Congress may have some delayed effect on public opinion through *ex post facto* inquiry, but as things now stand it can scarcely hope to influence policy in the formative stages. This is an area in which presidential decision, at least initially, is the crucial factor.

The President as Opinion-Maker

John F. Kennedy said he wanted to be President because that was the center of action. Vested in the presidency is not only the legal power to move and shake the federal bureaucracy, to treat with foreign heads of government and chiefs of state, and to command the awesome might of the armed forces. The presidency also has the extra-legal power to be listened to by a worldwide audience.

The President is news—what he does, what he says, when he picks up his dog by the ears, or even when he has a slight cold. He can pre-empt the airwaves and address a waiting nation (though in a landmark decision in 1970 the Federal Communications Commission said that if he did this very often, the networks would have to give his opponents time for rebuttal). He can submerge almost any other event in Washington by the simple expedient of calling a press conference. He can get an otherwise routine press release from one of the departments on page one of the metropolitan press simply by announcing it himself.

The President can also influence the kind and amount of news coverage he gets by controlling the setting in which he makes an announcement—whether at a casual press conference, a TV address to the nation, or an appearance before a joint session of Congress. He can raise or lower the drama almost at will. When it is raised high enough, either artificially or naturally, the President usually has been able to count on preponderant public and congressional support. Such was the case with President Truman and his program of aid to Greece and Turkey, President Eisenhower and the Taiwan Straits, President Kennedy and the Cuban missile crisis, President Johnson and the Gulf of Tonkin. A conspicuous recent exception has been President Nixon and Cambodia, perhaps an indication of the changing times. Even though a President's actions or policies may subsequently have been questioned, at the outset he has usually carried the day with both public opinion and Congress.

Beyond the natural tendency to close ranks and rally round the leader, an additional restraining factor is at work in Congress. This is concern over the possible consequences to the United States' international position through rejection or frustration of a presidential policy in time of tension or crisis. A president can put Congress in a difficult spot by announcing a policy and seeking legislative approval or implementation of it at the same time, with no viable alternative course readily available. President Truman announced the Truman Doctrine on the same dramatic occasion—a special message to Congress—at which he requested the Greek-Turkish aid program. He thus committed the United States in the eyes of the world and imposed on Congressmen who wished to disavow his stand a heavier responsibility than most of them were willing to assume.[3] President Eisenhower used a similar technique in securing passage of the Formosa and Middle East resolutions in 1955 and 1957, respectively. President Johnson followed much the same procedure with respect to the Gulf of Tonkin incident in 1964.

Indeed, Johnson was so much the master of this technique that unwittingly he may well have curtailed its usefulness for his immediate successors by resorting to it too often. In the period 1965–67, one of his consistent replies to congressional critics of his Vietnam policy was to read the text of the Tonkin resolution, recite the overwhelming vote by which it was passed, and challenge his opponents to try to repeal it if they did not approve its mandate.

His approach irritated some members of Congress, especially Senators who had voted for the resolution as an expression of support for the President in a specific circumstance and without expecting it to be used as the principal underpinning for a war involving half a million American troops on the Asian mainland. Many of these Senators, especially among the Democrats, had been deeply troubled by earlier resolutions of the Gulf of Tonkin type but had generally kept their doubts to themselves. They were concerned on two counts. First, some felt that such resolutions somehow detracted from the constitutional powers of the President as Commander-in-Chief, and of the Congress to declare war. Second, they felt that the President was taking unfair advantage of them by arm-twisting and persuading them to commit themselves to support unknown presidential actions in unpredictable circumstances in an uncertain future.

3. Malcolm E. Jewell, *Senatorial Politics and Foreign Policy* (Lexington: University of Kentucky Press, 1962), pp. 163–64.

Until the great debate over Vietnam, after passage of the Gulf of Tonkin resolution, Congress was inclined to give the President the benefit of the doubt. This is no longer true, at least in the Senate. The first time following the Tonkin affair that President Johnson asked for a broadly worded resolution of support was in connection with his trip to Punta del Este for the Latin American summit meeting in April 1967. The House gave the President what he wanted, but the Senate Foreign Relations Committee, unwilling to commit itself in advance to a long-range aid program for Latin America, so emasculated the resolution that the committee's version was angrily described by the White House as "worse than useless." As a result, a disappointed President went to Punta del Este without the pledge of support he had sought.

Whether or not the committee reacted wisely to the President's request is obviously a matter of opinion. I had occasion to discuss the incident some three years later with former Secretary of State Dean Rusk who made the following comment: "Congress can't have it both ways. If they want to share responsibility for our foreign policy they have to be ready to say in advance what they are willing to do."

Issues of this nature which involve the relationship of Congress and the President often highlight the struggle between the two for public opinion. The principal weapons which each uses are the media of mass communication.

Role of the Press, Radio, and Television

The *sine qua non* of political survival in Congress is to be reasonably well known to the voters of one's state or district. A few members, mainly from small constituencies, manage this by assiduous personal contacts; but by and large, publicity is the life blood of a politician. (On occasion, members have resorted to dubious means to manipulate the press to their own ends; Senator Joseph McCarthy of Wisconsin was a prime example.) There is a profound truth in the apocryphal tale of the Senator who did not care what was said about him so long as his name was spelled correctly. The reaction of the late Senator William Langer of North Dakota to the Senate vote on the United Nations Charter in 1945, though admittedly unusual, certainly illustrates the point. When asked why he opposed the Charter, he offered this explanation: "The vote was 89–2. If I had voted for the Charter, I would have been one among 90 and nobody would have paid any attention to me. I voted against it and my name appeared on the front page of every newspaper in the United States."

Since World War II, publicity has become steadily harder to get. As the interests of the American people in the world have broadened, so have the horizons of the newspapers, news magazines, and radio-TV networks. There is relentless competition for newspaper space and television time from coups d'état in Latin America, the birthpangs of nationhood in Africa, war in Asia, East-West confrontations in Europe, the bureaucracy in Washington, crime and riots in the streets, and a thousand other things.

Competition for space and time affects also the Washington press corps. Despite a reduction in the number of newspapers published in the United States, and despite a concentration of television stations in three major networks, the Washington press corps has nearly tripled since World War II. (In 1941 there were 634 correspondents accredited to the press, radio, and periodicals in the galleries of Congress; in 1970, there were 1,633.) One of the tenets of journalism is: "if there is no news, make some." If the Washington correspondent on Capitol Hill does not find, or make, enough news to compete with reasonable regularity with the turmoil in the rest of the world or the rest of the nation, he hears about it, in quarrelsome tones, from his editors. In consequence, a great deal of news is created where none would otherwise have existed.

So far as foreign policy is concerned, the relationship of news-hungry correspondents and publicity-hungry Congressmen has an inherent potential for mischief. It is an axiom of journalism that conflict is an important, if indeed not an indispensable, element of news. It is an axiom of diplomacy that conflict is to be avoided, or at least reduced in intensity, as much as possible. The press looks for areas of disagreement; the State Department looks, or ought to look, for agreement. Members of Congress are a third party of interest who, by their comments and actions, can do much to influence a given situation towards intensified or reduced conflict. In congressional relations with the press, the pressures are almost always in the direction of bringing about further conflict between the United States and a foreign interest, between the legislative and executive branch, or between different groups within Congress.

There is a fine line separating situations in which conflict is healthy and those in which it is destructive. Delicate judgments are involved in knowing when not to rock the boat and when the national interest requires that the boat be rocked. The point is that the press often loses sight of these considerations and, in any case, is frequently unable to deal with them adequately even if some of its more perceptive correspondents and editors are aware of them.

Reporters on Capitol Hill sometimes approach members of Congress with ready-made quotes: "Senator, do you think the administration is guilty of gross negligence in country X"? And sometimes the Senator will say what the press generously puts in his mouth. On occasion the relationship is more subtle, and a suggestion from a reporter may start a sequence of events resulting in legislation or in a new policy (or at least a new policy debate) in the State Department. Indeed, a reporter with good contacts in Washington is in a better position to influence policy than is his paper's editorial writer—not by slanting news but by manipulating the making of it. Sometimes this is done with a high sense of responsibility, sometimes with crude cynicism, or what is perhaps even worse, with naiveté.

A favorite device is to ask a member of one of the committee's on foreign relations a question along these lines: "Do you intend to question the State Department about military assistance to country B?" If the answer is "No," which is more often the truth than not, then the story that emerges is that the committee is either shirking its responsibilities or whitewashing the Department, even though the committee at that moment may be involved in three other undertakings of much greater importance. If the answer is "Perhaps," then the story is that the committee will "probe" military assistance to country *B*. The press almost never permits Congress to "study" a problem or to make a routine request for information. Congress almost always either probes or investigates.

Through presenting matters in this light, the press contributes substantially toward setting up an adversary relationship between Congress and the State Department. Some would argue that this is what the framers of the Constitution intended, but one inevitable result is to trigger a defensive reaction in the State Department, which in turn increases suspicions in Congress and an unnecessary spiral of conflict results. There are quite enough real sources of conflict in the conduct of our foreign policy without creating artificial ones.

Although the top correspondents and commentators of the networks are as perceptive a group of observers as can be found in the nation's capital, television reporters assigned to run-of-the-mill spot stories are much more inclined than their colleagues from newspapers to ask unsophisticated, provocative, or irrelevant questions. The competition is far more intense for air time than for newspaper space, and a TV reporter's mobility is limited by the impedimenta of camera and crew. As he has only a limited number of opportunities during the day to get a news story which stands a chance of being shown for a minute or two that night, he tries to frame the most dramatic question possible in an effort to elicit a dramatic answer in a short period of time.

The way in which the press, and especially television, reports an issue does much to shape the debate on it. There is, perhaps, an inevitable tendency to define issues in terms of sharp, clear alternatives when in fact the range of reasonable choices may be both narrower and subtler. This has been especially evident in the debate over Vietnam, in which the participants have been characterized as hawks or doves—a piece of journalistic shorthand which greatly oversimplifies both the issues and the positions of the contending parties.

One of the most mischievous parts of the press-congressional relationship is the use the press makes, or tries to make, of Congress as an instrument for doing the press' own work. If a correspondent cannot get the facts of a story out of the State Department, he may try to find a member of Congress or committee staff member to get them for him. Sometimes publication of the particular story is in the public interest; sometimes it is not. In either case it impairs the element of confidence in congressional-executive relations.

This problem is partly due to a noticeable tendency of the press to cover the world from Washington. Admittedly, this is much cheaper than maintaining correspondents abroad, but the fact is that correspondents in Washington are limited to three main sources for news—the United States government (including Congress), the diplomatic corps, and the international agencies. At least the first two sources usually have their own axes to grind, and are a poor substitute for on-the-scene reports from correspondents stationed abroad.

Perhaps the most damaging breaches of confidence are the leaks that come out of supposedly private or executive committee meetings. Sometimes they are deliberate, sometimes inadvertent. It is a curious commentary on how the press views the government that the Secretary of State can talk privately to most of the population of Washington except to the members of a congressional committee. He can go to the Pentagon, or even to the White House, without anybody lifting an eyebrow. But let him go to Capitol Hill, and television cameras are set up awaiting his exit even before he arrives. No Senator can leave one of these secret sessions without running a formidable gauntlet of questions. If he does not drop some tidbit, however innocent, he runs the risk of being ignored by the press in the future—and to be thus ignored is the beginning of the end for most politicians. Out of a dozen tidbits dropped by a dozen Senators who have attended a committee meeting, the press can piece together a pretty good account of what occurred. And then Senators will complain that the Secretary of State is not frank with them.

There is validity to congressional complaints that officers of the State Department are often more frank with the press in backgrounders and off-the-record conversations than they are with congressional committees. Perhaps one reason is that the press affords better protection to its sources. "I have really been shocked," one responsible member of the House Foreign Affairs Committee told me in the summer of 1970, "to see how some of my colleagues walk out of a closed meeting of the committee and tell the press all about it." There is no doubt in my mind that the committees of Congress could do a great deal to improve the consultative process if they would be willing to set up a system of effective sanctions to prevent leaks of this kind.

Some members of the Washington press corps are overworked, and some are inclined to be a bit lazy. Frequently they, or their editors, lack the knowledge, time, and space to put a story in its proper context. Nearly all of them expect to be given texts and other prefabricated handouts, on which they often base their stories and tend to ignore whatever extemporaneous debate may follow in the House or Senate, as well as whatever questions and answers may follow in committee hearings. This is probably one factor in the decline of extemporaneous debate. In addition, it gives the author of a handout—whether a speech in Congress or an executive branch statement before a committee—greater control over the content of news dispatches than would otherwise be the case.

Like Congress, the mass media not only reflect public opinion; they also help to create it. The traditional means of doing this, i.e., the editorial pages of newspapers, have become less important than interpretive reporting and, especially, less important than TV. Television influences public opinion not so much by the way it reports the news as by the fact that it reports it at all. A pictorial report or a short film of casualties in Vietnam or of street rioters in Washington certainly has a more profound impact than written descriptions of the same events. Indeed, news is sometimes made simply because a television crew is present; on occasion, it has even been instigated by crews looking for something to shoot. This is analogous to the newspaper reporter developing a dull-day story, but with television the impact is much greater. It is one of the great ethical and operational problems which neither the television industry nor the Federal Communications Commission has yet been able to resolve.

Lobbyists, Pressure Groups, and Constituents

Ultimately, the public opinion that matters most to a member of Congress is that of his constituents. The more heterogeneous his state or district, the more diverse this opinion is likely to be. In any case, its influence depends more on qualitative than quantitative factors; a vocal minority which feels intensely about a given issue will almost always carry the day against a more apathetic majority.

A Congressman tries to keep up with what his constituents are thinking through his mail, public opinion polls, personal visits, and the advice of trusted friends, political lieutenants, or party leaders in his home state or district. The volume of mail is impressive, even after allowance is made for the high content of junk. The Senate Post Office estimated in 1970 that it receives 17 million pieces of mail a year. This is 170,000 pieces per Senator per year, or roughly 700 per working day. On occasions of great public interest in an issue, the rate goes up by a factor of 10 or more. In the period immediately following the invasion of Cambodia in May 1970, mail was delivered to senatorial offices not in bundles but in sacks, and staffs fell weeks behind in even opening it, let alone sorting, counting, or acknowledging it. The Senate Office Buildings abound with stories of personal letters which were lost in the deluge, to be found weeks later.

Mail can be very deceptive, even when it is heavily one-sided. "I have 10,000 letters asking me to vote for the Bricker Amendment to the Constitution," said one Senator during that memorable debate, "but three million people voted in my state in the last election, and I have no idea how the other 2,990,000 feel." (The Senator voted against the amendment and was re-elected.)

The conventional wisdom around the Senate is that there are many ex-Senators who voted according to their mail. A great deal depends on how much time must elapse until the next election; the public's memory is notoriously short. And there are, of course, all kinds of mail. There is that which is spontaneous and that which is obviously inspired. Generally speaking, members of Congress pay little or no attention to inspired mail. Unless it is from their own state or district, they probably do not even bother to answer it. But personal, thoughtful mail makes an impression.

During my years on Capitol Hill I can recall only a few instances when mail on foreign policy questions made any heavy impact on the Foreign Relations Committee. One instance concerned the ratification of the U.N. Charter, when the flood of letters and telegrams made it unmistakably clear that the great majority of Americans in all walks of life strongly favored U.S. membership in the new world organization. If any serious doubts had been lurking in the minds of the committee, they should have been dispelled by that outpouring of popular sentiment.

A second instance had to do with President Truman's nomination of General Mark Clark to be our Ambassador to the Vatican. In this case, most experts in diplomacy would probably have supported the President simply because of the Vatican's role in world affairs and its importance as a listening post. But Protestant leaders had other ideas. Visibly angered at the prospect of our government establishing formal ties with the Pope, they played on anti-Catholic sentiment in the country and stirred thousands of Protestant congregations to action. The heavens opened and an avalanche of protest mail descended on Capitol Hill. As a result, the committee quickly dropped the nomination and President Truman withdrew it from the Senate.

Two observations are in order. In the first place, with respect to foreign policy, the forces of public opinion do not assert themselves very often in any concerted, organized way. The fact remains, however, that church groups and other organizations can exercise a tremendous amount of influence on policy-making if they choose to do so. Their potential, still in the embryonic stage, is very great indeed. In the second place, public opinion can be wrong—or at least illogical. In that event, Congress in its wisdom must decide where the emphasis should be, on logic or politics.

Once again the Greek-Turkish aid program is illustrative. It will be recalled that President Truman's surprise request generated much adverse public opinion. The mail opposing it was fairly heavy. Thirty-three nongovernmental witnesses asked the Foreign Relations Committee for the privilege of testifying on the proposal, and most of them vigorously opposed it. The Committee listed attentively to all, then after considering the evidence in secret session, unanimously voted to support the President.

Congressmen of course read the published public opinion polls. Some accept them as accurate; others are as skeptical as was President Truman. Some Congressmen even take their own polls. A Senator, especially from a large state, may order a poll made privately by a professional organization in preparation for a political campaign. Another kind is an unscientific straw vote in the form of a questionnaire which a Congressman circulates among a large number (not a scientifically selected sample) of his constituents. The questions are sometimes loaded so that the replies will show that the Congressman and his constituents are in close agreement.

Perhaps the indicator of public opinion on which Congressmen rely most is their own intuition fed by personal visits with constituents and the advice of political supporters.

Constituents are not simply a collection of individuals. The American public has a great penchant for organizing itself into chambers of commerce, garden clubs, labor unions, parent-teacher associations, professional societies, and associations for (or against) one thing or another. Most of them are given to passing resolutions on public questions. Most of the larger and more affluent also hire lobbyists to represent them in Washington.

Pressure groups acquire political significance in three principal ways: from the people they include (who may be important either because of their numbers or their identities), from their success in identifying their particular point of view with that of a larger public, and from contributions to political campaign funds.

If a lobbyist in Washington speaks on behalf of an organization with millions of members, that fact alone presumably means he is expressing the opinion of a substantial part of the public. Members of Congress are frequently skeptical as to how strongly the millions of members of a mass organization feel about the particular issue the lobbyist is discussing and tend to discount his views as those of a special pleader. To gain credibility, therefore, the lobbyist may try to sway Congress indirectly through influencing public opinion.

In its crudest form, this is the source of the inspired mail which fills congressional wastebaskets. In its subtlest form, it may be a great nationwide publicity campaign intended to have indirect results. It may be the supposedly spontaneous organization of a committee, which may sometimes be two or three degrees removed from the real source of funds and influence. On a foreign-policy matter, the real source may be a foreign government. Under the Foreign Agents Registration Act, nondiplomatic representatives of such governments are supposed to report their activities to the Department of Justice where the reports become a matter of public record. But in a careful investigation in 1962–64, the Senate Foreign Relations Committee found several loopholes in the Act. As a result, amendatory legislation was passed in 1966 to tighten the requirements on who must register and what must be reported.

Finally, pressure groups gain influence beyond the geographic area of their political base by contributing to political campaign funds. This is the source of much influence in areas where a particular pressure group would otherwise be weak.

Generally speaking, organized pressure groups have not had much influence on Congress with respect to broad questions of foreign policy. Their interests and their influence are usually limited to specifics—for example, sugar import quotas, aid for Israel, protection of American investments abroad. Sometimes the executive branch uses its own considerable influence to neutralize these interests, but frequently the pressure which Congress feels from private groups has in fact been inspired by the administration. Universities which have technical assistance contracts with AID respond to administration suggestions that they appeal to Congress not to cut foreign aid funds for technical assistance. Manufacturers of military equipment urge Congress not to restrict Defense Department programs for financing arms exports.

One Man, One Vote

Three recent developments are going to affect profoundly the different segments of the public with whom Congress is concerned. These are the heavy increase in Negro voting, especially in the South; the decisions of the Supreme Court in the reapportionment and redistricting cases; and the Court's decision on lowering the voting age to 18 in federal elections.

One cannot foresee in detail how these developments are going to affect congressional attitudes toward foreign policy. The civil rights movement, which is one of the principal causes and beneficiaries of these developments, has tended to become concerned with more than its original issues. Before his death, Dr. Martin Luther King was increasingly emphasizing the desirability of ending the U.S. involvement in Vietnam. His successors have followed much the same line. One reason, no doubt, is that it has become apparent that the problems of disadvantaged groups in the United States (of whom Negroes are the most numerous) are too profound and complicated to be solved by legal guarantees of equal rights and equal opportunities. Quite aside from the merits of U.S. policy in Vietnam, our involvement there is obviously diverting substantial resources which might otherwise be devoted to solving, or at least alleviating, the problems of the disadvantaged in the cities and the rural poverty areas of the United States.

One of the reasons the problems of the cities developed was that their residents, rich and middle class as well as poor, were grossly under-represented in state legislatures. Until very recently, the make-up of these legislatures has not changed to reflect the increasing urbanization of American society. Legislatures have continued to be dominated by rural interests which were reluctant to levy the taxes or carry out the programs needed by the cities. It has also been these malapportioned legislatures which have drawn the district lines for their states' representation in Washington. Congressional districts reflected the same rural bias that was present in the legislatures and so, as a consequence, has the House of Representatives.

Thus by the late 1940s the House had become more conservative than the Senate—a situation precisely the opposite of what the Founding Fathers intended. Most Senators served broader and more cosmopolitan constituencies. A Senator from a large mixed-economy state, like New York, Pennsylvania, Ohio, or Illinois, could not hope to be elected, no matter what his party, unless he ran well in the metropolitan areas where most of the votes were. And in order to win votes in New York, Philadelphia, Pittsburgh, Cleveland, Cincinnati, Chicago, and their suburbs, he had to appeal to minority groups and to industrial workers. However, his colleagues in the House from upstate New York, downstate Illinois, or rural Pennsylvania or Ohio were generally representing safe districts, which were basically conservative and changed little over the years except for a slow attrition of their population. The Representatives from these districts were ordinarily more conservative than the Senators from the same states; and, relative to population, they also outnumbered the Representatives from the urban districts of those states.

This difference between House and Senate began to show itself on foreign policy by the late 1940s in two major respects. First, the Senate tended to be considerably more liberal in matters of appropriations for foreign aid and for foreign operations in general. It is a characteristic of the appropriations process and applies across the board. "That's why," former House Republican Leader Charles Halleck from Indiana once remarked, "they call the Senate the upper body. It's always upping our appropriations." It is also why the House has sometimes irresponsibly cut appropriations against its better judgment, knowing the Senate would probably repair most of the damage, while the House could make a cheap political point by voting for economy.

Second, in the consideration of foreign policy the House as a whole tends to be more ideological—its heavy emphasis on anticommunism is illustrative—while the Senate tends to be more pragmatic in its approach. With the exception of the aberrant years of Senator Joseph McCarthy's era, the Senate, for example, has generally been more willing than the House to experiment in developing East-West trade and in building other bridges between the non-Communist and Communist worlds.

More recently the House has tended to be more willing than the Senate to approve the administration's foreign aid proposals, but it has been markedly more hawkish with respect to Vietnam and markedly more conservative with respect to East-West relations in general. The situation may reflect in part the increasing inward-looking, domestic orientation (some people call it neo-isolationism) of the urban-based civil rights groups mentioned above, though it should also be noted that some of the most eloquent Senate spokesmen for this point of view—Church of Idaho, Fulbright of Arkansas, Mansfield of Montana, and Aiken of Vermont—come from states virtually without cities.

In any event, it seems clear that the Supreme Court's series of one-man-one-vote decisions has set in motion a chain of events which sooner or later will significantly alter the shape and character of American politics. The full impact of these decisions will not be felt until at least the 1972 elections, which will reflect the results of the 1970 census. The changes wrought by the Court's decisions happen to coincide with the growing disorder in American cities, the rising debate over Vietnam, and the intensifying problems of the national budget deficit and balance of payments. All of these factors, taken together, point to an increasingly turbulent and uncertain public opinion, which may well lead Congress to become more domestically oriented and also more assertive of its prerogatives vis-à-vis the President, whoever he may be.

A third development that could have a profound impact upon Congress and its attitude toward foreign policy is the Supreme Court decision of December 21, 1970, upholding the federal law lowering the minimum voting age from 21 to 18 years in federal elections. Today over half the people in the United States are 27 years of age or under. During the 1970s over 11 million of these will normally be in the 18- to 20-year age bracket. Obviously all young people do not embrace the same principles and ideals, and all are not interested in world affairs. But they are less inclined to be influenced by the slogans and prejudices of the past than their parents or grandparents, and they will be confronted by challenges unprecedented in our history. If the high schools and colleges do their jobs reasonably well, the younger generation could drastically change the character of American politics by sending to Washington a new breed of able young legislators who just might take the lead in reshaping and revitalizing American foreign policy.

But steps taken to widen the franchise will not necessarily result in a better-informed electorate. More votes do not mean better votes. Public opinion polls still show a shocking lack of knowledge on the part of millions of Americans about some of the fundamental aspects of foreign policy. If people do not know the difference between Nationalist China and Mainland China, how can they possibly have enlightened views about our Asian policies? And if they know little or nothing about nuclear weapons how can they be expected to react intelligently when our government is trying to decide whether to proceed with the development of an anti-ballistic missile system? Ignorance, prejudice and apathy cannot be overcome overnight, and there is still a stupendous job to be done at the grass roots if the American people are to play their role well in the decision-making process.

At least two helpful trends deserve comment in this connection. In the first place, more and more members of Congress, by the frequent use of opinion polls, questionnaires, newsletters, and TV and radio programs, keep in fairly close touch with their constituents on both foreign and domestic issues. Even more promising is the growing number of members who return to their home states with increasing frequency to take part in face-to-face discussion meetings at the grass-roots level. In informal give-and-take of this kind they can not only keep abreast of public opinion, they can also exercise a greater degree of leadership than heretofore in the evolution of our foreign policy.

Although the political picture in the United States remains confused at this writing, this much is clear. As we move into the 1970s, two of the groups which have been most vigorous in their criticism of the establishment and of the values of the older generation—the new black voters and the 18–20 year old voters—now hold the balance of power in their hands if they want to use it. In 1960 John F. Kennedy won the presidency by the narrow margin of 113,000 votes. Eight years later Richard Nixon won with only 43 per cent of the popular vote. Given a little determination and the will to organize, the younger generation has enough voting strength not only to influence the shape of foreign policy, but to become the decisive factor in the presidential elections of 1972 and 1976.

Chapter VI

Foreign Policy, National Security, and Politics

Any observer of the congressional role in foreign policy has to be constantly on guard against the pitfalls of generalization and oversimplification. There are so many currents and cross-currents of attitudes and actions that it is deceptively easy to pick one out as representative of *the* congressional mood. Yet this mood varies from time to time and from issue to issue, and as it varies, the protagonists play different roles. In some respects, the scene is not much different from a psychedelic light show.

Attitudes in Congress toward foreign policy in general, and its proper role in particular, have been heavily influenced—one might say dominated—in recent years by the problem of Vietnam. It is American involvement in Vietnam that has led to increasing congressional preoccupation with the possibility of similar involvements elsewhere and, in turn, with the relationship between foreign policy and national security. But it has not led to any noticeable change in congressional attitudes towards U.S.-Soviet relations, which are, in the long-run, at the crux of American foreign policy. Nor has it led to noticeable changes in attitudes toward such trouble spots as the Middle East.

To confuse the picture further, members of Congress have changed their positions on an issue, as has the executive branch; they have supported the administration in one case and opposed it in another, neither voting for nor against the President consistently. In these respects the American system is working as it was intended to work—that is, with separate branches of the government coming independently to their own conclusions, which in some cases coincide and in others diverge. Let us review how this works in practice, taking three important problem areas as examples: U.S.-U.S.S.R. relations, national security policy, and the Middle East.

U.S.-Soviet Relations

The most fundamental and pervasive problem of American policy since World War II has been our relations with the Soviet Union, which, in one way or another, have affected almost all congressional actions on foreign policy. These actions, and the debates leading up to them, have reflected a fundamental ambivalence in American attitudes. There is a deep ideological antipathy to communism combined with a pragmatic desire to arrive at a *modus vivendi* with the other superpower. At times, one attitude has been ascendant; at times—not always far removed—the other.

In part, these irregular changes in our thinking have been caused by shifts in Soviet policy. Congressional attitudes have tended to harden or soften in response to the temperature and the velocity of the winds blowing from Moscow.

In part, varying congressional actions have resulted from lack of coordination in Congress. The issue of relations with the Soviet Union has almost always been presented in terms of specifics—whether to provide aid to a threatened country, to approve an arms limitation treaty, to authorize concessional sales of agricultural commodities to Soviet satellites, to support a U.N. peace force opposed by the Soviets, or to restrict or encourage trade with the countries of Eastern Europe. Because the general issue has such widespread ramifications, it has been a factor—sometimes determinative, sometimes marginal—in congressional decisions on a broad range of matters under the jurisdiction of at least a dozen committees besides Foreign Relations and Foreign

Affairs. Furthermore, the issue has frequently been raised in what would otherwise have been an obscure section of a bill of much wider application. Restrictions on Export-Import Bank financing of East-West trade were carried in a foreign aid appropriations bill. The requirement to suspend most-favored-nation treatment of Poland and Yugoslavia was part of another bill authorizing participation in the Kennedy Round of trade negotiations. In short, congressional treatment of issues affecting East-West relations has been a prime example of the effects of the fragmentation of committee jurisdiction and of the need for better over-all coordination among committees.

When all of this has been said, however, it remains true that over the past decade, the net thrust of congressional action has been toward closer, cautious cooperation with the Soviet Union. It has been most noticeable with respect to arms control and disarmament, especially the control of nuclear weapons. Congress has been much more reluctant to approve economic measures looking to increased trade with the Communist bloc countries. In fact, congressional initiatives in the trade field have usually been in the direction of making U.S. policy more restrictive. Congress has also been more hesitant than the executive on cultural exchanges with the Soviet Union, extension of consular relations, and the issuance of visas to visit the United States.

Quite apart from the question of direct U.S.-Soviet relations, a great deal of our postwar policy has been directed toward resisting the expansionist policies of the Soviet Union, and on many occasions the anti-Communist argument has helped to win congressional support for the foreign aid program and the collective security arrangements of the late 1940s and the 1950s. A part of the strength of the anti-Communist argument has been that it has given members of Congress an argument that they, in turn, could use with their constituents to justify their votes in favor of foreign aid.

One has only to review the legislative history of important policy issues like the Greek-Turkish aid program, the Marshall Plan, NATO, the Mutual Assistance Program, the treaties with

Germany and Japan, SEATO and other mutual defense treaties, and national defense appropriations generally to realize how compelling the anti-Communist argument has been. These and other related policies were sold to a receptive Congress as essential steps that would enable the United States and its Western allies to meet the challenge of Communist expansion. Indeed, whenever the executive branch ran short of logic it used the anti-Communist argument, which rarely failed to generate support on Capitol Hill.

On the other hand, as early as 1951, a resolution sponsored by the late Senator Brien McMahon of Connecticut was passed, expressing the desire of Congress and the nation for peace and friendship with the Russian people. As the cold war thawed following the death of Stalin in 1953, Congress normally supported political measures of coexistence.

In 1955, after years of what had seemed to be fruitless negotiations, the Austrian State Treaty was signed, ending the occupation of the four Allied Powers and recognizing Austria as a sovereign, independent (but neutral) state. The treaty was ratified with exceptional speed: it was transmitted to the Senate June 1, the Foreign Relations Committee held a hearing June 10, reported the treaty unanimously June 15, and the Senate voted 63–3 on June 17 to advise and consent to ratification.

In 1959, again after long negotiations, the United States and the Soviet Union joined ten other countries in signing the Antarctic Treaty neutralizing that area, banning nuclear explosions and radioactive waste disposal there, and guaranteeing freedom of scientific investigation and of unilateral inspection. The principal significance was that this marked the first time in the postwar period that the Soviet Union had been willing to agree to unlimited inspection. It also marked the first time the United States and the Soviet Union had agreed to formal, mutual limitations on the use of atomic weapons. After three days of debate, the Senate gave its advice and consent to ratification on August 10, 1960, by a vote of 66 to 21.

Ever since the 1940s the United States had been engaged in

what seemed endless negotiations with the Soviet Union on the general problem of arms control and disarmament. Although most of the discussions took place in a multilateral framework under the aegis of the United Nations, the principal parties were the two nuclear superpowers, and it was generally assumed that meaningful disarmament or measures of arms control rested on agreement between them. During these years Congress, especially the Senate, took an active and on the whole sympathetic interest in the problem. In July 1953, the Senate passed a resolution calling for "enforceable limitation of armament." In 1955, it created a special Subcommittee on Disarmament which, under the leadership of Senator Hubert Humphrey over the next several years, held a number of hearings and made some very useful studies. Also in 1955, the Senate passed a resolution endorsing a proposal to study the possibilities of limiting military spending with a view to improving world living conditions.

Carrying out a campaign promise by President Kennedy, Congress created the Arms Control and Disarmament Agency in 1961 as an independent agency whose director was designated as a principal adviser to the President and the Secretary of State. Congressional debate on this matter came during the Berlin crisis of September 1961 and immediately following Soviet resumption of nuclear testing in the atmosphere. These circumstances led in the Senate to an unsuccessful motion by Senator Dirksen to put off consideration of the bill until 1962, and in the House to criticism by Representative Thomas Pillion of New York that the bill was "another sign of our willingness to surrender." Nonetheless, the measure passed the Senate by a vote of 73 to 14, and the House by a vote of 290 to 54.

In May 1963, 34 Senators introduced a resolution asking that the United States offer the Soviet Union an agreement banning nuclear tests in the atmosphere and underwater but not underground. The purpose of this distinction was to avoid what seemed to be the insuperable difficulties of agreeing with the Soviets on means of inspection to enforce an underground test ban. There was considerable confidence (though not unanimous agreement) among the technical experts that atmospheric and underwater tests could be detected without on-site inspection.

The resolution had a helpful impact, principally because of the caliber and number of its sponsors, even though no formal action was taken on it. On June 10, the United States, the United Kingdom, and the Soviet Union announced that talks would be held in Moscow in July to seek agreement on a test ban. The talks moved ahead quickly, and the treaty (which did not apply to underground tests not venting radioactive debris beyond the borders of the country making the tests) was signed on August 5 in the presence of a delegation of Senators who had flown to Moscow for the ceremony.

There followed an historic Senate debate. Hearings began before the Foreign Relations Committee August 12 and lasted until August 27. Members of the Armed Services Committee and the Senate section of the Joint Atomic Energy Committee were invited to participate and did so. Simultaneously, however, the Preparedness Investigating Subcommittee of the Armed Services Committee held a separate series of hearings with emphasis on military and scientific testimony, though many of its witnesses were the same individuals who had appeared before Foreign Relations.

The two committees came to diametrically opposite conclusions. The Preparedness Subcommittee, in a report signed by six of its seven members, concluded that the treaty presented "serious —perhaps formidable—military and technical disadvantages for the U.S.," and that it was a matter of "personal philosophy" whether these were outweighed by the political advantages. On this point, the Foreign Relations Committee had no doubts. Its report stated:

> . . . This treaty does bear, though perhaps not heavily, on the military balance. But its thrust is political. And among other things, it illustrates that military considerations cannot be divorced from political considerations; they are inseparable, especially in the nuclear age. The maintenance of a strong military position is clearly essential to the national security of the United States. But exclusive, or excessive, reli-

ance on military considerations could undermine national security by encouraging comparable military efforts by others, thereby strengthening the destabilizing forces adrift in the world, possibly creating new ones.[1]

Here, in capsule form, are the opposing congressional views of the world and of the relationship between the military and political aspects of national power. It was, as the Preparedness Subcommittee said, a matter of "personal philosophy." In this and similar cases involving broad questions of U.S.-Soviet relations, the Senate accepted the "personal philosophy" represented by the report of the Foreign Relations Committee on the Test-Ban Treaty. But in a number of other cases involving the United States' own defense posture it was not willing to do so.

The Senate gave its advice and consent to ratification of the Test-Ban Treaty by a vote of 80 to 19. This was followed by the 1966 Treaty on Outer Space (approved 88 to 0 by the Senate in April 1967) prohibiting the establishment of military installations and the conduct of maneuvers on celestial bodies, providing that neither outer space nor celestial bodies should be subject to claims of sovereignty, and guaranteeing the right of inspection. The nuclear test ban also led to the resumption of U.S.-Soviet negotiations on a consular convention which was signed in Moscow June 1, 1964, and approved by the Senate on March 16, 1967, after almost three years of sporadic debate.

Parenthetically, this convention demonstrates how important minority party votes can be to the administration in a tight situation. The final vote was 66 to 28, only three more than the two-thirds majority required by the Constitution. Forty-four Democrats and 22 Republicans voted for the convention; 15 Democrats and 13 Republicans were recorded against it. Even if all the 59 Democrats present had supported the treaty, President Johnson still would have suffered a serious set-back in his efforts to build bridges to the East if it had not been for the help that came from the Republican side of the aisle.

1. Senate Foreign Relations Committee, *Report on The Nuclear Test Ban Treaty* (S. Rep. 3, 88th Cong. 1st Sess.), p. 26.

Finally, in the summer of 1968, after arduous negotiations, the Nuclear Non-proliferation Treaty was signed. Most of the non-nuclear powers of the world agreed not to undertake development of nuclear weapons in return for assurances of nuclear protection from the United States, United Kingdom, and U.S.S.R. It was approved by the Senate by a vote of 83 to 15 on March 13, 1969.

In Article VI of the Non-proliferation Treaty, each of the parties "undertakes to pursue negotiations in good faith on effective measures relating to cessation of the nuclear arms race at an early date and to nuclear disarmament, and on a treaty on general and complete disarmament under strict and effective international control." This was generally taken as a pledge by both the United States and the Soviet Union to proceed with the negotiations which shortly became known by the acronym of SALT for strategic arms limitations talks.

The Soviet occupation of Czechoslovakia in August 1968 led the United States to postpone the beginning of the talks. When the Nixon administration took office in January 1969, it naturally wanted to make its own review of the situation, and the Russians showed no sense of urgency. Talks finally got underway in Helsinki in the fall of 1969, continued in Vienna in the spring and summer of 1970, and were resumed again in Helsinki in the fall. In March 1971, they returned once more to Vienna.

In April 1970, the Senate gave a vigorous push to the negotiations through a resolution, on a vote of 72 to 6, recommending that "prompt negotiations between the Governments of the United States of America and the Union of Soviet Socialist Republics to seek agreed limitations of both offensive and defensive strategic weapons should be urgently pursued" and that "the President should propose . . . an immediate suspension . . . of the further deployment of all offensive and defensive nuclear strategic weapons systems, subject to national verification or such other measures of observation and inspection as may be appropriate."

At this point one might well ask whether it is helpful for the Congress to pass resolutions of this kind, in effect advising the President how he should handle a particular situation, or how he should proceed with negotiations. The answer must be equivocal. Sometimes it is helpful and sometimes it is harmful—and often the distance between helping and meddling is not very great. Certainly the Vandenberg Resolution, which put the Senate on record in 1948 as favoring the concept of regional defense arrangements, and which gave the President a green light to proceed with the negotiation of the North Atlantic Treaty, was most helpful. On the other hand, some congressional resolutions —including a good many on foreign aid and some on Middle East problems—have embarrassed the President and tended to undermine his position in dealings with other countries. Obviously the Congress should jealously protect its right to advise. At the same time it should exercise great care in second-guessing the President and should carefully examine all such resolutions in the context of our total foreign policy in order to make sure they do not have negative or undesirable effects.

Congress obviously has had more misgivings about economic relationships with the Soviet Union, and with Communist countries in general, than it has had about political relationships. In the depths of the cold war in 1951—the same year it passed the McMahon "friendship" resolution—Congress approved the Mutual Defense Assistance Control Act, popularly known as the Battle Act after its principal sponsor, Representative Laurie Battle of Alabama. This legislation sought to control the trade of U.S. allies with the Soviet bloc by withholding U.S. foreign assistance from countries trading with members of the bloc in various categories of restricted items—especially those commodities and materials that might help strengthen the military posture of the Communist nations. It was the obvious forerunner of even more rigid provisions inserted in the Foreign Assistance Act in 1963 and 1965 withholding aid from countries trading with (or even shipping to) Cuba or North Vietnam.

On October 9, 1963, scarcely two weeks after completion of

Senate debate on the Test-Ban Treaty, President Kennedy announced at a press conference that the Commerce Department would issue export licenses to private traders selling wheat, feed grains, and other agricultural commodities to the Soviet Union and other countries of Eastern Europe at the world market price. The decision followed a disastrous wheat crop in the Soviet Union and substantial Soviet grain purchases in Canada and other free world markets.

The President's announcement set off a lengthy congressional debate which went to the heart of U.S. relations with the Soviet Union. On the one hand, it was argued vigorously that any trade, even in agricultural commodities on cash terms, was a form of aid, which eventually in one way or another would help the Soviet Union and its leaders in their avowed designs to "bury" the United States. On the other hand, it was argued just as vigorously that honest trade helped one side as much as the other, and that the development of commercial contacts in non-strategic items offered one important means of breaking down the Soviet Union's isolation and of encouraging the forces of constructive change which some people discerned in the Communist states.

The kernel of the dispute was whether the forces of change were real or only apparent, whether efforts to encourage them represented a reasonable hope or a delusion, whether one viewed the cold war as an ideological struggle to the death or as primarily a conflict of national interests which could be adjusted peacefully over a period of time.

As with so many basic issues in Congress, this one was settled, at least temporarily, in a way which almost everyone could tolerate and almost no one really liked. The Export-Import Bank was forbidden to guarantee commercial credits for wheat sales to Russia unless the President found it in the national interest and so reported to Congress within 30 days.

The Foreign Relations Committee held hearings in 1964 and 1965 on East-West trade at which the business community generally supported trade expansion. The Johnson administration also proposed a number of measures aimed at expanding trade and building bridges to the East—measures which fell within the jurisdiction of the House Ways and Means Committee and the Senate Finance Committee. But expansion of the Vietnam war meant that most of these efforts had to be shelved, at least for the time being. In fact, in extending the Export-Import Bank's authority in 1968, Congress tightened trade restrictions even more; the Bank was forbidden to participate in any credit for purchases by a third party of goods ultimately to be used in a country furnishing assistance to North Vietnam (i.e., the Soviet Union and the East European states).

In summary, over the period since 1946, Congress seems to have kept reasonably well in step with the executive branch and the country at large with respect to U.S.-Soviet relations. Congress as a whole has been somewhat behind the executive branch on economic issues and in recognizing the changes that have been taking place in Eastern Europe during this period, though *some* members may have been considerably ahead. A substantial body of opinion in Congress, probably a majority, has been if anything a little ahead of the executive in urging tireless effort in tiresome disarmament negotiations. This is more evident in the Senate, which has approved ratification of every U.S.-Soviet treaty presented to it by fairly large majorities. If Congress has frequently seemed to be going first in one direction and then in another, that is partly because it is a collection of poorly coordinated, strong-minded individuals. But more importantly, it is because that is the way the White House and the Kremlin have moved as well.

National Security Policy

Part of the debate over Vietnam was concerned with whether in fact the United States had a commitment there; if so, how the United States became committed in the first place; and what was the nature and extent of that commitment. Was it true, as Secretary Rusk argued, that "keeping our commitment" in Vietnam was an indispensable element in maintaining credibility else-where in the world; or did involvement in Vietnam reduce our credibility and more particularly did it reduce our capability to meet other perhaps more important commitments?

From this point, it was but a short step to a generalized concern over the nature and extent of U.S. commitments worldwide. The concern was heightened by the alarming balance-of-payments deficit and our dwindling gold reserves, by growing budgetary and fiscal problems, and by increasing demands for the allocation of more national resources to domestic programs.

One manifestation of the concern was increasingly sharp scrutiny, especially in the Senate, of the hitherto sacrosanct Defense Department budget. In the summer of 1969, a Senate amendment to strike out the authorization for the antiballistic missile system failed passage by a tie vote, 50-50. A year later, opponents of the ABM were somewhat weaker, failing by a vote of 33 to 62 to eliminate the system entirely and by a vote of 47 to 52 to prevent deployment at new sites. However, they did succeed—surprisingly enough in the generally pro-Pentagon Senate Armed Services Committee—in forbidding expansion of the system as much as the administration wanted.

The debate over the ABM was accompanied by extensive debate over MIRV (multiple independently targetable re-entry vehicles) and the conversion of single warheads in missiles to multiple warheads. The heart of the issue was clear: how much is enough? But the MIRV question was closely related to the SALT negotiations with the Soviet Union. Would approval of the ABM and MIRV put our government in a stronger bargaining position *vis-à-vis* the Soviet Union, or would it result in escalating the arms race beyond any possibility of control?

In general, Congress supported the administration's strategic concepts, but not without a good deal of argument, especially in the Senate. The significance lay in the fact that there was argument at all. In earlier years the ABM and MIRV proposals would probably have passed the Congress in a breeze as part of the price we must pay to defend the United States and its allies and to contain the Soviet Union. As we moved into the 1970s, however, it became apparent that Congress was determined to put even the Pentagon's requests for defense spending under the most rigorous scrutiny.

As Senate Majority Leader Mike Mansfield summed up the matter in an interview in the fall of 1969: "It was a reassertion on the part of the Senate and the Armed Services Committee of their authority and responsibility." He pointed out that henceforth the Pentagon would screen defense projects more carefully, the administration would be helped towards legitimate economies, and the public would know that the Senate was not simply rubber-stamping Pentagon requests. At the same time Senator John Tower of Texas commented that the backbone for the anti-Pentagon drive was furnished by members of the Foreign Relations Committee who had a "completely different mentality" from the Armed Services Committee.[2]

Even from the House side there were clear indications that an old era was ending and a new one beginning. "There was a time," said Representative George H. Mahon of Texas, Chairman of the Appropriations Committee, "that any member of Congress would hesitate to vote against anything proposed by the Joint Chiefs of Staff because he might be subject to the charge of being soft on communism." As a result of the Vietnam war, he said, "that day is over."[3]

The most notable and methodical manifestation of congressional concern over foreign commitments came through the establishment by the Foreign Relations Committee in early 1969 of a Subcommittee on U.S. Security Agreements and Commitments Abroad. Chairman of the subcommittee was Senator Stuart Symington of Missouri, a former Secretary of the Air Force and the only Senator at that time serving on both the Armed Services and the Foreign Relations committees. Symington's purpose was to relate national commitments to national resources. One could not make an intelligent judgment about

2. *Washington Sunday Star*, Sept. 21, 1969.
3. *Washington Post*, Dec. 27, 1969.

the Defense Department budget, he argued, unless one knew the number and amount of IOUs outstanding over the world that might have to be honored by the United States.

Symington proceeded with his work through meticulous staff investigations abroad, followed by detailed closed-door hearings in Washington. It soon became apparent that a great deal more was involved than simply cataloguing the formal commitments expressed in the various security treaties to which the United States was a party. There was a host of other commitments— some express, some implied, some secret, some not—which involved the United States, or might lead to its involvement, in a thousand ways in countries around the world. In its efforts to encourage at least the appearance of free-world support for its policy in Vietnam, the Johnson administration had agreed to special payments for Filipino, Thai, and Korean troops in Vietnam. There were also secret military contingency plans with the Thais and unadmitted American participation in the war in Laos. In some countries, the sheer size of its military presence involved the United States at best in difficult problems of community relations near American bases, and at worst in domestic politics through identification with whatever government happened to be in power.

The political and economic price which the United States had to pay—or felt it had to pay—for military base rights in other countries was far from clear. Some foreign governments might well assume that a commitment had been made where none was intended. In some cases, also, foreign governments might be in a position to commit the United States against its will—a particular hazard in countries where there are joint-use bases or where U.S. nuclear weapons are deployed.

To make a reasonable judgment about the tangible and intangible prices paid for base rights, one has to know the purpose of the base, how it fits into over-all military plans for defense of the area, what alternatives are available, and what their prices are. In collecting intelligence data, one has to know something about the intelligence which is gathered, what it contributes to the over-all picture, and the available alternative methods of collection.

The military in general, and the intelligence community in particular—precisely because they are responsible for our national security—are prone to overemphasize the importance of any given facility or activity. Somebody wth more objectivity and detachment needs to ask if a given piece of intelligence is worth the risks which are run in acquiring it, or if a given military base is worth what it costs in both political and economic terms. Traditionally this function has been performed by the National Security Council, and the information on which the NSC bases its decisions is among the most closely held in the government.

With the establishment of the Symington subcommittee, Congress began asking many of the same questions itself on the ground that the answers were necessary to enable Congress to make responsible judgments about a wide range of issues, including the defense budget itself. Furthermore, it was argued, the Constitution did not intend that these matters be left solely to executive discretion; and congressional acquiescence in this one-sided arrangement had been a dereliction of duty which should have been corrected long ago. There were even some who maintained that not only did Congress have a right to know the full details of nuclear weapon deployment abroad, but also that deployment and the arrangements under which it was made ought to be subject to congressional approval.

Predictably, this view was not warmly embraced by the executive branch, and many congressional questions were answered incompletely, only after a long delay, or not at all. In the impasse over the congressional need and right to know about national security policy, each side had a point and each side gave a little, but not enough to satisfy the other.

The Middle East

It is worth examining American policy toward the Middle East briefly because here, as in no other part of the world, domestic political forces have played a dominant role completely without regard to party lines. While the American public is generally more in sympathy with the Israeli than with the Arab cause, the pressure on Congress stems mainly from the strong emotional attachment which American Zionists and the American Jewish community have to the state of Israel and from the political influence which they have in the United States. This influence, in turn, comes in part from their numbers and role in American life, in part from their substantial political campaign contributions.

On the other hand, the influence of the Arab community in the United States is understandably negligible. Paul Porter, a prominent Washington attorney, illustrated the point neatly with an anecdote about his appointment as President Truman's special ambassador to the Arab-Israeli peace talks in Geneva in 1948. "I won't tell you what to do or how to vote," Mr. Truman said to his new ambassador, "but I will say only this. In all of my political experience I don't ever recall the Arab vote swinging a close election."

The unique position which Israel holds in American political life was illustrated on March 19, 1971, when Israel's Foreign Minister, Abba Eban, appeared before more than 40 members of the Senate in order to defend his country's policy with respect to the withdrawal of Israeli forces from conquered Arab territory. This was not the first time that a representative of another country has taken his case directly to the Congress, but it is usually not done in such an open fashion and at such a high level. One Senate leader noted that it was an "unprecedented procedure" for a foreign minister "to come here and negotiate with the Senate" rather than to sit down with the representatives of the Arab countries and with U.N. Mediator Gunnar Jarring. That Eban was willing to by-pass the Department of State was undoubtedly due to the fact that he knew both he and his country have many strong supporters on Capitol Hill.[4]

4. *Washington Evening Star,* March 26, 1971.

Congressional attitudes toward the Middle East are perhaps the most dramatic example of congressional response to a vocal, well-organized, affluent minority in the face of a relatively indifferent majority. The executive branch, of course, has felt the same pressures and has responded in much the same way, though the response has been much less noticeable in the case of Republican administrations.

On several occasions since the establishment of the state of Israel in 1948, Congress has provided more foreign assistance for that country than successive administrations have requested. Since the 1967 six-day war, Congress has been increasingly insistent that the administration sell more sophisticated weaponry to Israel, preferably on easy terms of repayment. In the military procurement bill in 1970, Congress even gave the administration authority which it had not sought for unlimited arms sales to Israel.

The Middle East experts in the State Department have traditionally tried to keep American policy in the region in balance —that is to say, really, to keep it from being too openly pro-Israeli. They realize the special appeal Israel has for our people, but they also realize full well the strategic importance of the oil-rich Middle East and the need for our government to keep on reasonably friendly terms with 13 Arab states. In this, they have generally fought a losing battle with both the White House and Congress, despite the fact that they have had the strong support of the Joint Chiefs of Staff.

The Middle East thus presents a sharp contrast to Vietnam, where the executive branch has generally been hawkish and the Congress increasingly dovelike. Although it may well be true, as President Nixon has said, that the situation in the Middle East is more dangerous than that in Vietnam because it has more possibilities of a U.S.-Soviet confrontation, the Congress in general has been much more willing to risk it in the Middle East. Indeed, some members who are most vocal in their criticism of our policy in Vietnam justify that criticism in part on the grounds that the United States ought to husband its resources for exactly such a confrontation in the Middle East—should the need arise—where the danger is greater and the stakes higher.

Senator Fulbright's role in this would seem to some to be a double paradox. One of the severest critics of administration policy in general, he has been one of the most outspoken (and one of the few) congressional supporters of State Department's views on the Middle East. Moreover, as one of the Senators who feel that the United States is overcommitted in the world and who are most skeptical of some American commitments, he has nonetheless proposed an additional, and potentially far-reaching commitment in the form of a security treaty with Israel, something which successive administrations from Truman to Nixon have persistently shied away from.

The Fulbright proposal for a security treaty with Israel was more complicated than it appears on the surface. In the first place, it was predicated on a number of preconditions, the most important of which was an Israeli-Arab peace settlement along the lines of the U.N. Security Council resolution of November 1967. Fulbright reasoned that the power of the Zionist lobby and pro-Israel feeling in the United States was so extraordinary that Israel in any case had what amounted to a U.S. security guarantee and that so long as this was implicit rather than explicit, it was open-ended. This being so, he felt it would be desirable to make the guarantee explicit but conditional on certain behavior by Israel.

These seeming contradictions, however, are more apparent than real. There is nothing inconsistent in a Senator opposing the executive branch when he believes it to be mistaken and supporting it when he believes it to be correct. The fact that this is still done despite all the intra-governmental ill will generated by the Vietnam issue is an indication that the American system is working as it is supposed to and is a tribute to those who make it work.

This brief digression into Middle East policy was undertaken to indicate that despite the bitterness over Vietnam, despite the differences over the relative roles of the executive and Congress in making foreign policy, the line-ups change on each side of each important issue. Although the trend has gone far toward institutionalization of the issues between Congress and the executive, there is still diversity at both ends of Pennsylvania Avenue. This is as it should be.

Chapter VII

What's Past Is Prologue

Since 1965 it has been quite plain that there is no longer a national consensus about the role of the United States in world affairs. It is the principal difficulty underlying most of the debate about who should play what part in the making of foreign policy in this time of serious trouble for the United States.

The situation is full of ironies. Not the least of these is that it was Lyndon Johnson, the great devotee of consensus, who was at the presidential helm when the consensus broke down. Richard Nixon, faced with the unenviable task of retrieving the situation, has been trying hard to build a majority, which is something quite different from building a consensus.

Johnson's favorite quotation was from the prophet Isaiah, "Come, let us reason together." Nixon made "Bring us together" the motto of his administration, the slogan on a sign held by an Ohio girl at one of his campaign rallies. The themes are not really very different, and neither President found great success with them. The Nixon approach, on which all the returns are not yet in, was to de-fuse the situation, to "lower our voices," to appease the hawks with rhetoric and the doves with action. This was a subtle and complicated maneuver, and its chances of success were clearly set back by the move into Cambodia in May 1970. It was, in any event, sufficiently ambivalent to arouse suspicion among some of the hawks in addition to almost all of the doves.

Basically, both Johnson and Nixon tried to manipulate Congress, though they went about it in different ways. Johnson, who had large majorities of his party in control of both houses throughout his administration, used his well-publicized powers of persuasion, at first very skillfully and then with decreasing success. Nixon, who was confronted from the outset with the opposition party in control of both houses, went about his task through trying to elect more of his own people to Congress.

There is nothing wrong with either approach. Both are in keeping with the time-honored principles of the great game of politics. But both approaches came up against the hard fact that foreign policy demands a broader base of public support than does domestic policy.

The Need for Greater Consensus

The American political system is designed to resolve differences through election: one side wins and the other side loses, and the winner goes on to enact his program while the loser nurses his wounds and prepares for another day. But the election of 1968 settled nothing, except to prove what everybody already knew, namely, that the country was seriously divided. The winning presidential candidate received substantially less than half of the votes and only a bare percentage point more than the runner-up. The American people voted for a Republican President, a Democratic Senate, and a Democratic House. In the most glaring contradiction of all, the majority in Arkansas on the same day voted for George Wallace for President, Winthrop Rockefeller for Governor, and J. W. Fulbright for Senator.

The result is political stalemate. When the processes created by the American system to resolve differences between the parties do not result in solutions, the system is stymied. But at the same time that the stalemate is the result of the failure of political processes, it is also—and more importantly—the cause of this failure. In other words, we have reached a political impasse and may be approaching a constitutional impasse, precisely because we are ourselves so deeply divided over what we want to do in the world.

The debate over whether dissenters should operate within the system or outside of it is in some respects irrelevant. The system itself presupposes a large measure of agreement. When agreement is totally lacking, as was the case in 1861, the result is civil war. When it is largely lacking, as was the case at the beginning of the 1970s, the result is friction, turmoil, and something approaching political paralysis.

It would therefore seem clear that, whatever view one may take of the proper constitutional function of Congress in the making of foreign policy, as a practical matter Congress has an important role in developing and reflecting a national consensus. Strengthening the congressional role is likely to result in a more viable foreign policy, if for no other reason than that it will command broader public support, based on a broader national consensus.

It has been the habit of presidents throughout our history, and of none more so than Johnson and Nixon, to argue that their foreign policies will work if they receive the strong support of a unified people. The negative formulation of the argument is a good deal more persuasive: foreign policies will *not* work if they do *not* receive the strong support of a united people. But this side of the coin is on occasion as invisible to the White House as the dark side of the moon.

Public support alone is obviously not a sufficient condition for a successful policy. A further condition is that the policy make sense in the context of the problem to which it is addressed. It is a fundamental mistake to assume that our foreign policies will work if they get support at home, and to reason from this premise that if they do not work it is because they do not have that support. From this fallacy it is but a short step to a greater one, namely, that vocal opposition in Congress is somehow insidious or unpatriotic or wrong. What this assumption overlooks is the possibility that the opposition might conceivably be correct and the policy mistaken.

The root of these fallacies lies in the policy-making process itself. Although some of the more portentous of American decisions (e.g., the reaction to Soviet missiles in Cuba) necessarily have to be made in secret, the basic American view of the role the United States should play in the world has to be formed in public. This is so simply because of the kind of society we have.

President Johnson was inclined to blame many of his problems on his critics in Congress who, he believed, were encouraging public dissent at the expense of the posture of unity with which he fervently wanted to address the Vietnam problem. In this, he was partly correct. There is no doubt that the hearings of the Senate Foreign Relations Committee in 1966–68 provided a forum for dissent, gave dissent more respectability than it would have otherwise had, encouraged it, and dramatized the divisions within the country.

But the other side to the controversy is of equal, perhaps even greater, importance. A good many Senators who were prominent dissenters in 1966 and later had held their tongues in 1964 and 1965—precisely out of respect for the President's argument that the policy would work if it had public support. They gradually became convinced, some sooner than others, that it would not work under any circumstances. More importantly, it should be noted that the congressional dissenters probably did not create public opposition so much as they reflected it.

This leads to a central question which will no doubt be debated for years to come. Did the Senate render a useful service in opposing the Vietnam War, or did its failure to support the administration make a bad situation even worse? Would the nation have been in a better position in 1970 if the Tonkin consensus has persisted and if Senators had not raised pointed questions about the Dominican crisis, and developments in Vietnam, Cambodia, and Laos?

We are unlikely to have a definitive answer to this question until the archives of the North Vietnamese government are available or at least until historians have been able to put the developments of the late 1960s in fuller perspective. Meanwhile honest differences of opinion will continue. "History will show," one official very high in both the Kennedy and Johnson administrations told the writer in 1970, "that Senate liberals were the primary reason the North Vietnamese wouldn't negotiate."

If the country is clearly divided over an issue, it is more in keeping with the American system that the differences be thoroughly discussed in public than that frantic and unsuccessful attempts be made to paper them over. Even though it might be argued that the protests in Congress have contributed substantially to the divisions in the country, it could be more cogently argued that these divisions are only going to be resolved by a process of national debate and of national soul-searching, and that there is no better forum than the Congress for the process.

Congress, however, has clearly gone beyond its role as a kind of national town meeting and is re-examining, as it has not done in modern times, not only its fundamental powers but also its duties and responsibilities in the making of foreign policy. In doing so, it has necessarily stepped on many toes and stirred up much resentment in the executive branch.

There is an important distinction to be made here between *making* and *conducting* foreign policy. Nobody seriously questions the pre-eminence of the executive in conducting foreign policy. As a practical matter, the conduct of foreign policy can be done only by the President or his agents, and furthermore, Congress has little stomach for the day-to-day details. Thomas Jefferson put it well during his term as Secretary of State: "the transaction of business with foreign nations is executive altogether." The *making* of foreign policy is quite another matter.

On the Making of Foreign Policy

In the first place, although the United States is a government based on the separation of powers, the making of foreign policy is in fact a shared power. It is shared principally by the President and the Senate, though since World War II as money and politico-military matters generally have become more important, the role of the House has grown considerably. For a shared power to be exercised effectively, those who share it have to be pulling in more or less the same direction.

In the second place, although in most cases the difference between making and conducting policy is clear enough, there remains an area of twilight, which has increased as the United States has become more involved in other parts of the world. Moreover, this twilight area covers a broad spectrum of policy issues. The fundamental question involved is how far the executive branch can, or should, go in implementing on its own authority a basic policy in the making of which Congress has not shared? And do various acts of implementing one policy commit the United States willy-nilly to another?

For example, in the ratification of the network of multilateral and bilateral security treaties in the Far East in the 1950s, the Senate endorsed, at least by implication, a network of American military bases in that area as well as a generalized American policy of resisting Communist expansion. Did this endorsement constitute sufficient authority for the executive branch to proceed to encourage and pay for military operations in Laos and to subsidize the maintenance of Korean, Filipino, and Thai troops in Vietnam?

The North Atlantic Treaty is another example. In approving NATO, the Senate endorsed participation in the joint defense of Western Europe and, by implication, the deployment there of American nuclear weapons. It did not endorse any particular level of such weapons, nor especially any particular arrangements for their deployment. Yet the secret executive agreements under which nuclear weapons are deployed, and which the executive branch has withheld from Congress, might well have a serious impact on the future problems of American foreign policy— problems with respect to which Congress might some day be called upon to act as co-pilot in a crash landing without even having known about the take-off.

These examples could be multiplied almost endlessly. American military bases may be established abroad to carry out a policy approved, at least implicitly, by Congress. But these same bases may give rise later to additional foreign policy problems which were unforeseen (whether they should have been foreseen is another matter) at the time the bases were established. The tendency of the executive branch is to deal with a great many of these additional problems without further reference to Congress except perhaps for money.

One of the thorniest problems in the twilight area between the making and conduct of policy is the difference between a treaty and an executive agreement. The difference has never been satisfactorily defined, and, indeed, even the unsatisfactory definitions change from one time to the next. When the original agreement was made with Spain in 1953 for American air and naval bases in that country, nobody in the Senate raised a serious protest that it should have been in the form of a treaty. To be sure, some Senators expressed doubts about its wisdom, but not about its legality. But when the agreement was renewed in 1970, there was a considerable, although largely ineffectual, outcry in the Senate that it should have been a treaty. The difference lies not so much in the nature of the agreement as in the fact that in 1970 a significant part of the Senate was far more sensitive about the implications of foreign commitments than it was in 1953. Despite persuasive legal arguments on both sides of the question at both times, the controlling fact was a basic difference of view over the substance of the issue.

If one thought, as the executive branch and part of the Senate did, that renewing U.S. rights to air and naval bases in Spain was in the national interest, perhaps even vital to national security, then one was likely to conclude that it was a matter appropriate for an executive agreement. On the other hand, if one thought, as some members of the Senate did, that the bases in Spain were a waste of money, not essential to the national interest, and likely to involve the United States in Spanish politics, then one would probably conclude that the whole matter should be submitted to the Senate as a treaty—where those with similar views would be in a better position to block it.

In point of fact, the decision to proceed through an executive agreement or through a treaty is usually made by the executive, based on criteria involving a curious mixture of legal abstractions and practical politics. The executive branch made a treaty with Mexico for the return of stolen archeological objects, but used executive agreements to arrange with Spain for a large American military presence in that country, and with Korea for the payment of a billion dollars in one form or another for the maintenance of two Korean divisions in South Vietnam. Usually there are sound reasons for decisions of this nature, but some of them are just weird enough to cause members of Congress to shake their heads in disbelief.

What the Role of Congress Should Be

Granted the existence of a twilight zone between making and conducting foreign policy, we must push our inquiry beyond what *is* to what *should be*. Most of this book has tried to describe the present role of Congress, and how it is changing under the pressure of events and of evolving attitudes toward the position of the United States in the world. It is time now to consider briefly what that role ought to be. Three points stand out:

First, Congress ought to bring to bear on foreign policy questions an informed judgment of its own, arrived at more or less independently of the executive branch.

Second, it ought to come to this judgment in public, with the benefit of open debate and discussion, in which representatives of the executive as well as private citizens participate.

Third, it ought thereby to contribute to the development of as broad a national consensus as possible in support of the policies eventually arrived at.

These points, in turn, raise a number of other basic questions. What is the precise relationship between the constitutional power of Congress to declare war and the constitutional power of the President as Commander-in-Chief to use our armed forces in military activities abroad? Whatever the framers of the Constitution might have intended, *can* Congress perform the role which has been outlined above in the context of international crises in the latter part of the twentieth century? And, whatever its role is or should be, how can Congress perform it better?

It has been argued in many quarters that modern weapons technology has made the war power of Congress obsolete. In the traditional sense, this is almost certainly so. Whether Congress likes it or not, its declaration of war against the Axis Powers in December 1941 may well have been the last occasion on which it exercised that power in the traditional way. As things now stand, a full-scale war, which could only come with the Soviet Union, or possibly in the future with Communist China, probably would come so quickly that as a practical matter Congress could have little or nothing to say about it—at least at the outset.

This does not, however, answer the difficult question of American troop deployments overseas, including troops engaging in hostilities, as in Korea from 1950 to 1953 and in Vietnam since 1965. There are at least 125 instances in American history in which Presidents have sent American troops abroad, often for combat purposes, without a declaration of war or any other kind of formal congressional approval. The weight of these precedents is frequently cited by the executive branch as establishing beyond question the right and authority of the President to do so. There is a distinction to be made here between the President's *right* and his *authority*. The armed forces of the United States are well disciplined, and within reasonable limits they will do whatever the President tells them to do, including fighting an undeclared war in Korea or South Vietnam. This is not to say that the President has the *right* to order them to do so, but only that he has the *authority*—always assuming that Congress does not forbid it, which the Senate came within nine votes of doing with respect to Vietnam in the summer of 1970.

There is also a distinction to be made between a declaration of war and less formal congressional action specifically authorizing troop deployments abroad, including combat. At the time of the interventions in Korea and Vietnam, no great outcry was raised in Congress, but both actions later became highly controversial. In both instances there were some sound reasons for not seeking a formal declaration of war. Such an action has a finality to it which would have seriously jeopardized our relations with the Soviet Union as well as with certain friendly countries, and would have made it far more difficult to prevent the spread of hostilities later on. The same objection, however, does not apply to forms of congressional approval short of a declaration of war. President Johnson thought he had such approval in the Gulf of Tonkin resolution but, as later events indicated, he was obviously stretching the congressional intent. In both the Korean and Vietnamese cases, it could be argued that Congress implicitly gave approval through appropriating money to carry on the war, but this is begging the question. Once American troops are committed to combat, it is in only the most extreme circumstances that Congress would even consider cutting off funds for their support.

In all probability both Truman and Johnson could have won congressional approval for their commitments of American troops in 1950 and 1965, respectively, though the latter case is somewhat less certain. Such support undoubtedly would have strengthened their positions later on, but more in a legal than a political sense. A large part of Congress and of the public obviously changed their minds about the two wars in the light of subsequent events. There is no satisfactory way for a President to protect himself against this eventuality.

Nor is there any satisfactory way to protect the national interest from aberrant behavior on the part of Congress, acting either in conjunction with, or independently of, the executive. The theory of the Constitution is that such aberrations are much less likely to occur if separate, independent actions are required —that is, both the Congress and the President are less likely to do something foolish at the same time than either is to do it independently.

Much is to be said for the theory, but it necessarily means at least a brief, perhaps a prolonged, delay—possibly even beyond the moment when armed action would be practical. One's attitude toward the constitutional question involved here again tends to be influenced by his attitude toward the substantive policy. If one comes, even retrospectively, to the conclusion that the intervention in Vietnam was a mistake, he is likely also to take the view that congressional approval should have been sought. This is on the (perhaps subconscious) premise that Congress would have checked the President in one way or another.

The premise is far from having universal validity. Supporters of a strong congressional role, for example, might argue that the President should have presented the Cuban missile crisis of 1962 to Congress. But if he had done so, who knows what the result would have been? He might very well have been confronted with a demand for more vigorous action than the situation justified. It does not follow that Congress is always and necessarily more prudent or more restrained than the President.

When all this is said, however, it does seem that for both constitutional and practical reasons, the executive branch should take Congress into its confidence more frequently and seek explicit approval for more of its major foreign actions. The executive is loath to do this because it would be a bother, involving much time, energy and patience. From the executive point of view, it would result at best in some delay and at worst in frustration. Moreover, there is a natural reluctance on the part of any president—and especially his advisers—to relinquish any of the powers which have been accumulated by his predecessors over the years. The fact that Congress is becoming more insistent on what it conceives to be its prerogatives is a reflection not only of its disenchantment with the executive branch, but also of the mood of the country.

In the end, the argument over the role of Congress in foreign policy comes down to an argument over the role of the United States in the world, over national priorities, and about the kind of country Americans want to live in. The heart of the argument over congressional participation in the making of foreign policy involves the relative prerogatives of Congress and the President.

The reason there is an argument is only in part due to built-in institutional jealousies. It stems much more from the fact that there exists a fundamental difference in view between the legislative and the executive branches.

This difference has been most dramatic in the case of the Vietnam war, but it goes considerably beyond that. Lyndon Johnson took the first step toward de-fusing the war in Vietnam in his now famous speech of March 31, 1968. President Nixon made some further progress with his enunciation of the Guam Doctrine and the policy of Vietnamization, though he suffered a setback with the unpopular intervention in Cambodia.

Nixon also set off new and heated disputes in his advocacy of the anti-ballistic missile and over his proposals for new, and fantastically expensive, weapons systems. The space program and the supersonic transport likewise came under increasing fire in the Congress and in the press, with the SST being rejected entirely.

All of this controversy reflected a debate over national priorities as well as divergent views throughout the body politic over the interests of the United States and how they should be defined. It has not been the purpose of this book to deal with the question of priorities and national interests, but with the context in which they are considered and debated and the procedures by which they might be resolved.

In the end, however, they can only be resolved through the working out of something like a broad national consensus. If there had been general agreement during the past decade on the course the United States should be pursuing, there would be no problem of the congressional role, or of legislative-executive relations, of more than academic interest. But there has not been any such agreement. The real question is whether it can be found.

In addressing this question, it is extraordinarily difficult to separate substantive and procedural views. Congress itself is divided, not only over Vietnam, but also—among other things—over the Middle East, over what new weapons systems are required for the national security, and over the feasibility of building more bridges between the East and West. People who generally support the administration are likely to find Congress a tiresome, quarrelsome nuisance, inefficiently organized and unable to cope with the problems of the modern world. People who generally oppose the administration's approach are likely to view Congress as the last, best hope of saving American democracy from the encroachments of a powerful executive. Both sides of the argument are apt to overlook the prospect that in other days, in other circumstances, the roles are likely to be reversed. Undoubtedly this is one of the considerations for which the system of checks and balances was set up.

The controversy over means and ends gathered new momentum once again as the Ninety-first Congress ground to a halt on January 2, 1971, battered by a massive wave of adverse public opinion. Critics were quick to castigate the Senate especially as an archaic body, inefficient and cumbersome, and tied up in knots for many weeks before coming to final action, or a decision to postpone action, on an array of important legislation including aid to Cambodia, funds for the supersonic transport, import quotas, foreign aid, and national defense appropriations. On the other hand, supporters of the Senate argued that what happened during the year was "the Senate's glory, not its shame"—that legislative impasses and delays were the direct result of important policy issues. These difficulties, they contended, stemmed largely from the fact that the Senate, for the first time since the war, was attempting to exercise independent judgment on national defense and foreign-policy questions instead of rubber-stamping everything requested by the executive branch.[1]

In looking at foreign policy from the congressional point of view it may appear to some that I have put too much emphasis on the importance of Congress at the expense of the executive branch. This has not been my intention. In working out a satisfactory relationship Congress must remain the junior partner.

Let me put the problem another way. Every day more than

1. See *The Washington Post*, Dec. 25, 1970; *The Sunday Star*, Dec. 27, 1970.

1,000 cables go out of the Department of State, many of them carrying instructions to embassies and missions all over the world. Every year the United States participates in more than 600 international conferences dealing with a whole range of problems from nuclear power and arms control to trade relations, labor questions and development in the new countries. Every hour steps are taken and decisions reached that shape this nation's destiny in the field of foreign relations. Now what is the role of Congress in all this? Obviously it must be limited. It can debate and criticize. It can challenge. It can review and amend. It can block action. It can even take the initiative with respect to certain policy decisions. It can, by persistent opposition, bring about important changes in our foreign policy—as it did in South Vietnam. But it has neither the time, the patience, the machinery, nor the capacity to take an active part in the day-to-day conduct of foreign policy. That must and will remain the task of the President and the executive branch.

It is not my purpose to derogate from the authority of the President. As Dean Acheson reminds us: "The central question is not whether Congress should be stronger than the President, or vice versa, but how the Congress and the President can both be strengthened to do the pressing work that falls to each to do and to both to do together." [2]

Improving the Flow of Information

How can this be done? Clearly one way to improve the quality of congressional participation in the policy process is to improve the flow of essential information to Capitol Hill. Information is the life blood of responsible action. So long as Congress remains poorly informed and relatively isolated from the executive it is destined to play an anemic role. Once the channels of information are improved, once Congress is kept better informed, it can again take over its full responsibilities under the Constitution.

This is not to say that if there had been a steady flow of infor-

2. *A Citizen Looks at Congress* (New York: Harper & Row, 1957), p. 56.

mation to the Senate on the Vietnam question, all members of the Senate would have seen eye-to-eye with the administration. Nor is it to say that the President would have been persuaded to pursue another course. In a free society there is always room for dissent. The point is that Congress is made up of reasonable men who will normally respond to a foreign-policy issue in a reasonable way, provided they have access to the same information that is available to officials in the executive branch.

There can be no doubt about it; our system of government suffers from the fact that meaningful debate on foreign policy questions cannot normally take place in Congress, as presently constituted. The House, which is big and unwieldy, is simply not equipped for effective debate. In the Senate, where a great forum for free discussion is available, those who could contribute most to the debate—notably the Secretaries of State and Defense —are conspicuous by their absence. Time and again in response to questions put to them, Senate leaders are forced to admit their lack of information on policy matters. "I regret that I cannot answer the distinguished Senator's question," is the oft-repeated refrain, "but I am not in possession of all the facts. The Senator should address his enquiry to the President." Or, "I am very sorry: I do not know what the administration has in mind. Perhaps the Senator would get a satisfactory answer if he would consult the Secretary of State." Appearance of cabinet officers before Congressional committees meets the problem only partially.

Obviously one way to help build up the Congress as a forum for foreign policy debate would be to invite the Secretary of State and the Secretary of Defense to appear at regular intervals on the floor of the House and Senate to answer questions on this country's foreign relations. This could be done by a simple change in the rules of the House and Senate and would not, in my judgment, alter either the letter or the spirit of the principle of the separation of powers. It would, in effect, borrow some of the features of the "question hour" procedure that have worked successfully in the British House of Commons.

For the "question hour" to succeed, certain safeguards would have to be established. Questions would have to be submitted in advance, so that satisfactory answers could be prepared. Moreover, neither of the Secretaries would be expected to answer questions involving the disclosure of classified information or questions that are otherwise contrary to the national interest.

It can be argued, of course, that if Cabinet officers were invited to participate in House and Senate debates in this fashion, they would exercise too much power and influence and would quickly rise to a position of dominance in the legislative branch. This is not a sound argument. In the limited question-hour arrangements referred to above, Cabinet officers would appear only at stated intervals; they would not sit on congressional committees, and they would not exercise the right to vote. In the circumstances, it is difficult to see how they could dominate the Congress—especially in view of the fact that many members are skilled in the rough-and-tumble of debate and could give a good account of themselves in any exchange of views with the executive branch.

A modest step in this direction was taken on March 25, 1971, when Secretary of State Rogers met with 67 members of the Senate for an extraordinary exchange of views on the administration's Middle East policy. The closed meeting represented one of the few times in recent years that a Secretary of State appeared before the full Senate. The meeting, which was apparently successful in clarifying the American position on the withdrawal of Israeli troops from conquered Arab territory, as well as other related matters, could serve as a precedent for future discussions with the Senate on important foreign policy issues.

An even more helpful step that could be taken to bridge the information gap between Capitol Hill and the White House would be the creation of a Joint Executive-Legislative Committee on National Security Affairs. The Committee would be made up of the President and the Vice President and some of their senior officials (including the Secretaries of State, Defense and Treasury, the Chairman of the Joint Chiefs of Staff, the Director of the CIA, the Chairman of the Atomic Energy Commission, and the President's Special Assistant for National Security Affairs), as well as leading members of the House and Senate (including the Majority and Minority Leaders, the Whips, and the Chairmen and ranking members of the Committees on Foreign Relations, Armed Services and Appropriations), some twenty in all.

The Joint Committee—which would be serviced by a small staff drawn from Capitol Hill and the executive branch—would meet at regular intervals for a full exchange of views on the important issues facing this country in foreign policy and national security affairs. It would not make formal decisions. It would not usurp the President's authority to command the armed forces and conduct foreign policy. Nor would it undermine the jurisdiction of the committees of Congress which have traditionally dealt with foreign affairs. Its workability, of course, would depend largely on the personality of the President.

With respect to the development of close ties, both Congress and the executive are about as shy as two teen-agers who have not yet had their first date. But the advantages that would flow from a joint committee of this kind are convincing:

1) Consultation would take place at regular intervals, so that congressional leaders could be kept abreast of important developments in various parts of the world.

2) Emerging problems could be flagged in advance, so that some of the crash decisions that have characterized our policy in the past could be avoided.

3) Because the President would seek their advice regularly, congressional leaders would have a more constructive role to play in the formulation of foreign policy.

4) Congressional debate would be improved inasmuch as the leaders on Capitol Hill would be far better informed both on matters requiring legislative approval and on foreign policy generally.

I am not suggesting, by this proposal, that opposition to the government's policies be muted or that congressional criticism be curtailed. It is obvious, however, that a reasonable degree of executive-legislative teamwork with its built-in opportunity for the clash of opposing points of view would not only be in the national interest, but would also strengthen our constitutional system at a time when it is in real danger of breaking down.

Has not the President often met with congressional leaders before on important issues? Of course he has. But the traditional White House briefings have been arranged, organized, and run by the executive branch with precious little opportunity for active congressional participation and even less time for a full exchange of views. As a result, many members go back to Capitol Hill somewhat better informed perhaps, but with their prejudices reinforced and their noses out of joint. On some occasions these one-way briefings have boomeranged, generating ill will instead of the cooperation they were designed to promote.

There remains, of course, the danger that the President, after consulting with congressional leaders, might repudiate their advice and take some action which they vigorously oppose. This is a risk the President always runs when he seeks advice from Congress; it is inherent in the consultative process. But if the President seeks advice only when he knows the answer will be favorable to his point of view, he will run into serious congressional opposition sooner or later.

Besides improving the consultative process there are at least two other steps that could be taken to help restore good working relations between the Congress and the executive. The first lies in restricting somewhat the use of executive agreements as instruments of foreign policy. The second lies in the development of some reasonable understanding between the two branches about the President's use of American forces abroad.

Before turning to these suggestions, one rather obvious point should be made about the short run, and that has to do with the war in Vietnam. In recent years this has been a constant source of misunderstanding, irritation, ill-will, and bitterness. Once the was is over, once the principal seat of infection has been cleared up, the chances of developing a more healthful working relationship between the ends of Pennsylvania Avenue will be greatly improved.

Restricting the Use of Executive Agreements

First, the problem of executive agreements. It is my conviction that sincere efforts should be made by the executive branch to be more discriminating in the use of executive agreements, especially in the highly sensitive area of national security affairs. In 1970 only 16 treaties were submitted to the Senate for its consideration. Executive agreements are easier to conclude and easier to terminate; and the tendency is to conduct more and more of American foreign policy through them, rather than through treaties. This is in part due to the great expansion of our international relations since World War II, but it is also due to deliberate attempts by the executive branch to by-pass the Senate and the discouraging two-thirds vote required for the ratification of treaties.

It would be misleading to suggest that all executive agreements are entered into without congressional consent. Some are made pursuant to legislative authorization—AID legislation and the Trade Agreements Program, for example—in which Congress has delegated certain authority to the executive branch. Some are for the purpose of implementing treaties already approved by the Senate. But a good many are concluded under the authority of the President as Commander-in-Chief, head of the national administration, and the official charged with responsibility for the conduct of foreign policy.

NATO offers an interesting example of a kind of Parkinson's Law whereby international commitments expand in a fantastic ratio to the original treaty or legislative base. Actually the North Atlantic Treaty is a very simple one of 14 short Articles by which the contracting partners agree to maintain and develop their individual and collective capacity to defend themselves against armed attack. Yet since 1949, when the treaty went into effect, NATO has evolved in a remarkable way, with an elaborate command structure, a highly developed infrastructure including transport and communications facilities, and detailed plans for the defense of Western Europe. I am convinced that not one of the Senators who voted to approve the treaty was then able to foresee, even in the wildest stretches of his imagination, this kind of development. And most of it was accomplished by executive agreements.

Those fearful of the abuse of presidential power must keep in mind that they are handling a two-edged sword. The fact is that the executive heads of most governments today have the power to act promptly. We certainly do not want to curtail the President's authority to the point where he is seriously handicapped in his dealings with other countries. This is precisely why the Bricker Amendment to the Constitution went down to defeat in the Senate; it proved impossible to draft a proposal that would eliminate the risk of serious abuse and still retain for the President sufficient power to enable him to carry out his executive responsibilities. The Senate refused to jump from the frying pan into the fire.

On the other hand it would seem equally foolish to permit a proliferation of international obligations by executive agreements which Congress, in its wisdom, might see fit to repudiate later on. There is, after all, a certain element of insecurity about executive agreements which make them less desirable than treaties for important and long-range commitments.

Indeed, one can argue that the two-thirds vote requirement for treaties has compelled a certain amount of bipartisan cooperation that has been most helpful in the postwar era. Commitments like the U.N. Charter, the North Atlantic Treaty, and the Rio Treaty are not "one shot" propositions. They need the continuous support of Congress year after year, regardless of the party in power. Ever since the U.N. Charter was ratified, Congress has been called upon annually to approve a wide range of activities related to the United Nations. The continuity of this support can only be assured if the basic treaty has been approved by an overwhelming vote.

One problem we face stems from the stubborn fact that no Solomon has appeared to work out a satisfactory classification of international agreements—which ones should be submitted to the Senate in treaty form, which should be sent to both houses of Congress, and which can be put into force by the President acting on his own authority. In this situation the policy of the executive branch should be aimed at two objectives: (1) to avoid deluging Congress with a mass of trivia which it is not equipped to deal with; and (2) to invite congressional participation in all agreements in which the legislative branch has a legitimate interest. Where there is any doubt about the latter objective, consultation between the two branches should provide a reasonable answer.

The War Power

Finally, some step should be taken to meet the obvious and legitimate congressional concern over the President's power to use the armed forces abroad in limited and undeclared wars. Consultation with the executive branch as it is now conducted is not enough. Certainly, experience has demonstrated that the power of the purse, to appropriate funds for the maintenance of armed forces, is not a very effective way for Congress to exercise its control over undeclared wars. Rightly or wrongly, many members are convinced that Congress must devise some method of asserting and establishing its authority at the beginning of hostilities.

In the postwar period we have neatly side-stepped any attempt at precise definition of the President's authority to use American forces either generally or in support of our international commitments. With respect to the latter, we have made clear that any action that might be taken to implement the various collective defense treaties the United States has entered into must be in harmony with our constitutional processes. This means, in effect, that the nature of the American commitment has been obscured, leaving for the future the decision in each case whether and under what circumstances force might be used and the relative roles of the President and the Congress in deciding it.

The North Atlantic Treaty is a classic example of this deceptive but reassuring formula. Article Eleven comfortingly provides that the treaty should be ratified "and its provisions carried out by the Parties in accordance with their respective constitutional processes." Did this mean that the President, on his own authority, could take whatever action he deemed necessary to repel an armed attack against the NATO defense area? Did it mean that he could defend Copenhagen and Paris with the same power and authority that he might use to defend New York and San Francisco? Not at all. It simply meant that any action taken by our government to meet an armed attack under the treaty—whatever that action might be—would be taken in accordance with our normally accepted constitutional practices and procedures.

Moreover, the Foreign Relations Committee did not consider it appropriate in 1949 to define the President's authority to use the armed forces. "The treaty in no way affects the basic division of authority between the President and the Congress as defined in the Constitution," said the Committee in its report. "In no way does it alter the constitutional relationship between them. In particular, it does not increase, decrease, or change the power of the President as Commander-in-Chief of the armed forces or impair the full authority of Congress to declare war." [3]

When John R. Stevenson, State Department Legal Adviser, testified before a subcommittee of the House Foreign Affairs Committee on July 1, 1970, on the subject entitled *Congress, the President, and the War Powers*,[4] he pointed out that the decision-making process in foreign policy should be aimed at giving maximum fulfillment to five principal objectives: (1) it should enable this country to respond quickly; (2) it should permit secrecy prior to the use of armed forces where secrecy is required

3. *Senate Executive Report* No. 8, 81st Congress, 1st Session.
4. Hearings Before the Subcommittee on National Security Policy and Scientific Developments (Washington, 1970).

for the success of the operation; (3) it should provide a means of taking decisive action which reflects a national determination; (4) any decision to use armed force should be based upon a maximum amount of information about the nature of the threat and the consequences of the action; and (5) it should ensure that the type and amount of force used is adequate to meet the danger posed.

These are all valid and important considerations and, as Mr. Stevenson suggested, "the process of decision must strike a balance among them." [5] Here is the crux of the matter. How can a proper balance be struck between the need for a secret and speedy decision and the other ingredients in the formula, especially those relating to an informed and representative decision-making process? Supporters of presidential authority contend that such a balance cannot be prescribed in advance by formal legislation. Rather, it must be worked out in practice as each situation arises. The main thing, the argument runs, is to avoid so restricting the President by legislation that the United States cannot respond quickly and effectively to emergencies. As Professor James MacGregor Burns has put it: "In a world of unstable equilibrium, Executive discretion and power must be seen as one more weapon for stability—a weapon of response, of adjustment, of intervention." [6]

To the objective observer it would appear that a reasonable balance can and should be struck. The point is, the flood of resolutions introduced in the House and Senate indicate not only a keen desire but a determination on the part of a good many thoughtful members to retrieve for the Congress at least a modest portion of its forfeited war power. The avowed purpose of the resolutions is not to criticize or assess blame or to penalize future Presidents for the mistakes of the past. The real purpose is to carve out a more realistic relationship so that, in the words of Congressman Clement J. Zablocki, Chairman of the House subcommittee, the two branches of government "might act as

5. Hearings, cited, pp. 209–10.
6. Hearings, cited, p. 82.

partners, moving in concert toward the greater national interest." [7]

Congressional concern is by no means limited to the so-called dove group or to those who have traditionally opposed the expansion of presidential authority. The Zablocki subcommittee, for example, after completing its hearings on *Congress, the President, and the War Powers,* reported out a mild resolution which imposed no restrictions on the President's powers, but required him to submit written reports to Congress on the commitment of American armed forces in foreign lands. The resolution was later approved by the House. Even more significant as indicative of changing sentiment is the January 20, 1971, speech of Senator John Stennis, long one of the Senate's principal supporters of the President's powers as Commander-in-Chief. Stennis called upon Congress to exercise its constitutional role in a more vigorous fashion and announced that he was striving to develop a realistic approach to the problem that would recognize the President's authority to repel an attack on American forces, but would require congressional approval "before hostilities can be extended for an appreciable time." "Only by a decisive vote in the Congress which represents the people," he went on to say, "can there be a real test of the sentiment of the country for supporting any war and mobilizing all our resources."

The resolution introduced by Senators Javits and Dole, referred to above, is a useful example of what some people believe could be done without doing violence to our constitutional system. It would make clear the power of the President to take action in order to repulse any sudden attack against the United States and to meet certain other emergencies. It would, however, require the President to secure congressional approval within 30 days, in the event action beyond that time limit proved necessary. Thus the President would be able, under the resolution, to act speedily and decisively to defend the national interest. But for military action of a longer-range character, the approval of Congress would be required.

7. Hearings, cited, p. 5.

* * *

It will be noted, in the suggestions outlined above, that most of the changes in the direction of establishing better relations would be initiated by the executive branch. This does not mean that Congress is entitled to sit by and do nothing. The very least it should do is to overhaul its out-moded machinery so that it can assume a partnership role more responsive to the needs and the challenges of the 1970s.

Congress is a deliberative body. No one, so far as I am aware, has ever argued that rapidity and dispatch and efficiency are among the major virtues of a representative assembly. Congress does have the facilities, however, to serve as a forum, a national sounding board, where the major issues of foreign policy can be thrashed out and where the nature and purposes of American policy can be critically examined. If these facilities are properly organized, Congress can be of inestimable value in helping to shape the difficult policy decisions that face our country in the years ahead.

The events of the last decade, including the Vietnam war, the Cuban missile crisis, the deepening chasm of suspicion and distrust between mainland China and the U.S.S.R., the ominous rumblings of discontent in Eastern Europe, the growing independence of our Western allies, the expanding aspirations of the new countries, the intensification of the Middle East crisis, and the threatening spiral of nuclear armament—combined with our own domestic problems—have injected a new fluidity, a new uncertainty into our world relationships. They raise, in a new and sharper form, the basic motives and directions of American foreign policy.

It is obvious that the winds of change are blowing over Capitol Hill and over the country, bringing some fundamental reappraisals of American policy. We need answers to such questions as: What is the nature of the Soviet or Communist threat in the circumstances of the 1970s and how can we best meet it? What should be the nature and scope of American commitments abroad? How far should we go in exercising our power and

influence in helping to keep peace in the world? Do we need a
new set of priorities between domestic and foreign affairs, and
among various aspects of the latter?

We have reached a point where we are ready to move in the
direction of developing a new national consensus and of laying
the basis for a new foreign policy. With the President actively
engaged in the day-to-day conduct of foreign affairs, Congress
can be of great assistance, just as it was during and after World
War II, in helping to find suitable answers to these difficult
questions.

When Woodrow Wilson wrote his classic book, *Congressional
Government* in 1885, the political pendulum had swung far in
the direction of Capitol Hill. Wilson pictured the Congress as a
despot with "unlimited time" and "unlimited vanity"—a despot
that had "virtually taken into its own hands all the substantial
power of government." He complained, too, that consultation
with the Senate had a tendency to be a one-way street. "The
President really had no voice at all in the conclusions of the
Senate with reference to his diplomatic transactions . . ." he
wrote, "and yet without a voice in the conclusion there is no
consultation." [8]

Under our system of government there is room for the pendulum to swing between the executive and legislative branches as
it has done on a number of occasions since the days of Woodrow
Wilson. At this juncture it appears to be swinging once more
toward Capitol Hill where a restless and assertive Congress
seems determined to stop the erosion of legislative authority and
to restore at least some of its constitutional prerogatives in the
conduct of our foreign policy. In periods in which there are
great differences among the American people over what they
really want to do about world affairs, a swing of the pendulum is
not only inevitable, it is a good sign our system is working. But
we must never forget there are built-in limitations on how far
it can and should swing.

8. Woodrow Wilson, *Congressional Government* (Boston: Houghton Mifflin
Co., 1913), p. 45: See also Acheson, cited, p. 63.

In some ways the Constitution of the United States is an invitation to disunity in the field of foreign relations, and in a free society a certain amount of disunity can be endured. "Error of opinion may be tolerated," Thomas Jefferson once reminded us, "where reason is left free to combat it." For most Americans, however, it is not a reassuring spectacle to see the President and the Congress seriously at odds over an important policy issue when the nation's vital interests are at stake.

The two need not remain seriously at odds. Although they may differ from time to time, both must seek a common ground in ways by which the misunderstandings and their legitimate differences can lead to constructive ends. What we need in the 1970s is a greater willingness on the part of both the legislative and executive branches of our government to work together for the common good.

Index

RECENT PUBLICATIONS

FOREIGN AFFAIRS (quarterly), edited by Hamilton Fish Armstrong.

THE UNITED STATES IN WORLD AFFAIRS (annual), by Richard P. Stebbins.

DOCUMENTS ON AMERICAN FOREIGN RELATIONS (annual), by Richard P. Stebbins with the assistance of Elaine P. Adam.

POLITICAL HANDBOOK AND ATLAS OF THE WORLD, 1970, edited by Richard P. Stebbins and Alba Amoia (1970). SUPPLEMENT (1971).

THE REALITY OF FOREIGN AID, by Willard L. Thorp (1971).

JAPAN IN POSTWAR ASIA, by Lawrence Olson (1970).

THE CRISIS OF DEVELOPMENT, by Lester B. Pearson (1970).

THE GREAT POWERS AND AFRICA, by Waldemar A. Nielsen (1969).

A NEW FOREIGN POLICY FOR THE UNITED STATES, by Hans J. Morgenthau (1969).

ATLANTIC AGRICULTURAL UNITY: Is it Possible?, by John O. Coppock (1966).

TEST BAN AND DISARMAMENT: The Path of Negotiation, by Arthur H. Dean (1966).

COMMUNIST CHINA'S ECONOMIC GROWTH AND FOREIGN TRADE, by Alexander Eckstein (1966).

POLICIES TOWARD CHINA: Views from Six Continents, edited by A. M. Halpern (1966).

THE AMERICAN PEOPLE AND CHINA, by A. T. Steele (1966).

INTERNATIONAL POLITICAL COMMUNICATION, by W. Phillips Davison (1965).

ALTERNATIVE TO PARTITION: For a Broader Conception of America's Role in Europe, by Zbigniew Brzezinski (1965).

THE TROUBLED PARTNERSHIP: A Re-Appraisal of the Atlantic Alliance, by Henry A. Kissinger (1965).